Stay Positive

daily reminders from
Positively Present

Danielle DiPirro

Table of Contents

HAVE AN ATTITUDE

Positivity

January 1

Cop an attitude. A *positive* attitude, that is. Your attitude is one of the few things you have total control over. Sometimes life limits your choices, but life never limits what kind of attitude you can select. Choosing a positive attitude will change your life. It will infiltrate every aspect of who you are, what you do, and where you go. You have the power to change what you experience by changing how you think about those experiences.

January 2

Positivity takes practice. Like anything worth doing, it doesn't come easily. You will have to work on it constantly—and the more you work, the better you'll become at pointing out positive aspects of any situation. Encourage yourself to be optimistic—even if it might seem forced at times—and, much to your surprise (and delight!), you will actually *become* optimistic.

January 3

There is something positive in everything. In every person, in every situation, there is something good. Most of the time it's not obvious. You have to look. And sometimes you have to look *hard*, really squinting to see that shining glimmer of goodness. But it's always there. Just keep looking. Positive things are all around and if you take the time to look, you will always find what you seek.

January 4

If you want to live a positive life, you must surround yourself with positive people. Do not allow those with pessimistic attitudes and negative actions to crowd your positive space. You, as much as anyone, deserve to live a positive life. And you cannot accomplish that great feat with negative people around you. Separate yourself from those who stand in the way of optimism.

January 5

Share your wealth of positivity with the world. The best way to do this is quite simple: be nice. Be nice to other people, no matter what. Tell someone she or he looks nice today. Tell someone he or she did a great job on that presentation. Tell your loved ones how great they are. When someone is feeling down, do what you can to cheer him or her up. Send flowers. Write notes. Don't gossip. Be kind to all living things. *Share* your positivity.

January 6

You can make great strides toward living a more positive life by learning how to frame your thoughts and ideas positively. By using language with positive connotations and selecting affirmative words, you can write a positive perspective of the world. To cultivate positive language, you must think before you speak and learn to be more conscious (and conscientious) about the words you use.

January 7

Positivity isn't simply cheerfulness. Cheerfulness can be a cover-up for what's really going on beneath the surface, but positivity is an internal belief that allows you to focus on the good in any situation. Positivity can, but doesn't always, lead to cheerfulness. Cheerfulness can be, but isn't always, a sign of a positive outlook. If you want to live a positive life, you must learn not just to be a *cheerful* person, but also to be a *positive* one.

January 8

It can be very hard not to be dragged down by others' negativity, but you have the power to control your own attitude. No matter what others do or say, you have the ability to choose a positive mindset. You have the capability to shape your world (and possibly theirs) with your own optimistic thoughts and actions. Do not let others drag you down. Instead, strive to lift them up.

January 9

When you're going through a tough time, the last thing you usually want to do is embrace a positive attitude. When faced with negative emotions, it can be hard to see through the rain clouds to a time when the sun will once again be shining. However, looking past those clouds to a brighter, better day is exactly what you need to do when times are tough. Acknowledging the clichéd-but-true notion that things *will* get better will transform whatever you're going through into a situation you can cope with.

January 10

Whatever you look for in life, you move toward. The attitude you have when you wake up will permeate your entire day. If you start off with a positive attitude, you'll be more aware of the good things that happen. Likewise, if you start off negatively, you'll be drawn to see the negative things that occur. When you recognize that what you focus on, you move toward, you realize that beginning each day positively is just that much more important for having a good day.

January 11

Negativity is too easy. Surrounded by so much negativity in mainstream media, it's seems simpler to give into the judgments and pessimistic points of view held by so many. But if you are thinking negatively, you are taking the easy path. You are doing what is average. And *you* deserve more than average, than the easy path. Push yourself toward a positive point of view.

January 12

Don't let one bad thing ruin your positive attitude. When the bad seems overwhelming and it's taking over your thoughts, pause and think about what positive things can be taken from this bad situation. What else in your life is making you happy? How much good is there compared to this one bad thing? Just one bad thing can have a lot of power—and it can destroy a positive attitude if you let it get the best of you. Don't. Choose to shift your focus and find the good.

January 13

Being negative gets you nowhere. There is nothing to be gained from looking at the negative side of things. While the positive may, at times, seem idealistic, it forces your brain to think about the world optimistically and increases positive emotions and actions. Thinking negatively, on the other hand, does not. It does nothing good for you, so why do it?

January 14

Don't fool yourself into thinking positivity is something you had to be born with. It can be learned. (It can also be taught.) If your nature isn't inherently positive, don't worry. You can still *choose* positivity. You may have to work a bit harder than some, but you will get there. Don't give up on yourself. There is a positive force within you—and it's up to you to dig down deep and access it.

January 15

Negativity can be hard to escape. Not only must you contend with your own mind, but also you must deal with those around you who can project negativity. You face pessimistic environments or situations, and you have to deal with depressing images in the media. But there are many ways to avoid negativity. Whether it is removing yourself from a situation or taking the time to think about your own positive viewpoint, finding ways to combat negativity is an essential step for embracing a positive life.

January 16

Optimism is not a form of denial. Positivity does not mean pushing away anything that doesn't make you happy. Instead, it is the belief that there is always a silver lining. It is the knowledge that, no matter how bad things might seem, there is something good amidst the pain and heartbreak and unhappiness. Positivity is courageous. It is brave. Do not let others tell you otherwise.

January 17

Here are three things you could do today to create more positivity in your life: (1) do something that engages you, (2) practice a random act of kindness, and (3) forgive those who have hurt you. You can do one (or all!) of these things right now. Today. Positivity shouldn't be paused. It should always be playing, making itself known through words, thoughts, and actions.

January 18

Pay attention to your negative beliefs. What do you think of in a negative light? Who do you view as a negative person? Look closer. Dig deeper. Is that negativity really valid or could there be a positive perspective you're choosing not to see? There is often more than meets the eye when it comes to black-or-white judgments. Look for the gray areas, the possibilities for positivity.

January 19

Slippery slopes are not limited to negative landslides. Positive momentum can also gather quickly and propel you in a new direction. One positive thought can begin an avalanche. How can you build that momentum in your life today? What one thing can you do right now to trigger that avalanche of optimism?

January 20

Spread positivity with acts of kindness. Acts of kindness shouldn't be random. You shouldn't do them every once and awhile. You should do them all the time. You should treat kindness like it is limitless and free (which it is!). The smallest thing—a smile, a kind word, a door held open— can spark positivity. It can blaze a fire in someone else that will light up the rest of the day. You have the power to fan these positive flames wherever you go. One kind act is all it takes.

January 21

Positivity is not naïve. Positivity is necessary. Many believe possessing a positive attitude during difficult times is a sign of idealism. Being positive doesn't mean you're naïve or indifferent or impractical; being positive means you have the strength to stand up to a negative situation, to courageously refute negativity and embrace the good in what's happening now (even if that now seems pretty rough).

January 22

Little bits of negativity will creep into your mind from time to time. And you know what? That's okay. Being positive doesn't mean being positive *every second* of every day. It means making the most of a situation to the best of your ability and trying to see the good, even when that's very difficult to do. Positivity isn't perfect. Positivity is always a work in progress.

January 23

Clear your heart and head of negative thinking. Ridding your life of negativity will open up space for more positive things. Positivity—and the choice to surround yourself with positive activities and people—will create more time for you to do the things you love. It will open up space in your heart for new beliefs and experiences.

January 24

A positive attitude allows you to be more centered in the now. By going into a situation with a positive attitude, you'll be more interested in it and more fully aware of what's happening. Because of this, you'll be able to expand your ideas of what you find enjoyable because you'll be giving new things a chance. You'll engage in activities and situations you might never have before. A positive attitude can lead to an adventurous life.

January 25

Every single day, every single second, you have a choice: you can assume a positive attitude or you can assume a negative one. And, amazingly, every moment is a chance to start again. If you didn't wake up in the best mood, do not be disheartened. You can start again right now. Your attitude is always open to alterations. Nip and tuck whenever necessary. Tailor your thoughts to be positive.

January 26

There are more than two boxes simply labeled NEGATIVE and POSITIVE. Try to avoid placing anything in a single box. Labels—even good ones—tend to limit the way you see the world. When you encounter a negative situation, person, or attitude, question it. Ask yourself if there is, beneath the surface, something good. You will often be surprised by the positive attributes you find when you start looking for them.

January 27

Sometimes you will find yourself holding on to negative beliefs that are near and dear to you. You will ignore positive perceptions of situations or people because you don't want to let go of what you've always known to be true. Open your mind to optimism when it comes to tightly held beliefs—even those you've carried around for a lifetime—and you'll free yourself from the chains of negative thinking.

January 28

Just as choosing the right accessory can significantly influence the look of an outfit (in a good or a bad way), so too can your attitude significantly impact your day. When you wake each morning, you can choose what type of attitude will accessorize your day. Is it always easy to reach for positivity? No. It's often a difficult choice to make. But in stretching yourself, reaching for the harder choice, you'll transform the way you look—and the way you see.

January 29

No matter how tough things are, there is at least one thing going right in this moment. It might be a small thing—like your ability to still get out of bed in the morning or the sun shining lazily in the sky—but the size of it doesn't matter. What matters is that it's there. Instead of focusing on the negative, direct your attention to the things (however small) going right. Make it a game if you must (Spot the Positive Thing!), but seek to spot the good things—even when life's hard.

January 30

How often do you encounter a friend, coworker, or relative moaning about how bad a situation is? While it's important to sympathize with others, it's also important to help others see the positive in negative situations. The next time someone comes to you with a whine or complaint, remind him or her about the good that comes with the bad (and, yes, *every* situation has a bit of good in it).

January 31

Positivity often gets a bad rap, with positive people discredited and labeled "Pollyannaish." Be open to having a positive attitude. Positivity is not silly or frivolous, naïve or unintelligent. Positivity is a bold choice in the face of the negativity surrounding us. Positivity is a challenge—but it's one that you're up for.

IT'S WHO YOU KNOW

Relationships

February 1

Relationships are necessary for living a positive life, but cultivating positive relationships is no easy feat. A lot stands in your way when it comes to creating a thriving connection—and that's why you must take care of your relationships. You must tend to them as the fragile and delicate things that they are. Do not take positive relationships for granted. Do not waste emotional energy on pessimistic people.

February 2

Emotions have a ripple effect on relationships. Your emotional state can impact those around you, and the emotional states of others can impact you. Consider how you let your emotions infiltrate your relationships and ponder whether or not you are surrounding yourself with positive emotions. Also, do not forget that those you spend time with greatly impact your emotional state. Choose your friends wisely.

February 3

Relying 100% on just one person is a big no-no when it comes to having positive relationships. Don't focus all of your attention on that one special person in your life (no matter *how* special he or she seems). Nurture relationships with many different types of people and each of your relationships will flourish.

February 4

Negativity has the tendency to creep not only into your thoughts but into your relationships as well. When you feel overwhelmed or stressed by a relationship, take a time out and consider all the things you enjoy about that person. Contemplate their good traits—even if those traits aren't so apparent in the moment. Make room for positive thinking in your relationships.

February 5

No matter what you would like to believe, you have little control over others. Realize this and you will free yourself from a lot of mental anguish. Though you may be able to influence others at times, you generally cannot control what others think, say, or do. Do not strive to control others, but instead focus on how you can control your reactions to what they say and do.

February 6

Sometimes it's difficult deal with others' behaviors and it can be more difficult to separate yourself from these behaviors. Sometimes you may feel so close to a person that you consider him or her to be part of who you are—but other people do not make up who you are. Who you have relationships with is not who you are. You are your own person with your own identity. You are connected to others, but never forget that you are an individual.

February 7

You can improve relationships with others by not caring about what they do. You can both remove yourself from caring about specific actions and still care about the person. Not caring is a great way to improve a difficult relationship with someone you love. By not caring, you can stop trying to change those around you. You can fully accept others for who they are and, as a result, be at peace with the choices they make.

February 8

Most relationships contain conflict. But conflict is not necessarily a bad thing in moderation. Conflict is a great way to learn more about others. If you pay attention, you will learn not only about another's point of view, but also about the way he or she argues. If you pay close attention, you can pick up a lot of information about others when you actively engage in conflict. Do not shy away from it; strive to engage in conflict positively and productively.

February 9

What you love—and don't love—about others can show you a lot about who you are and what you value. Consider the people you are closest to. What do you love most about them? What don't you like so much? Why? Instead of simply interacting with those you see on a daily basis, spend some time thinking about what attributes about those people appeal to you. Being aware of these traits can help you have a better understanding of your relationships.

February 10

Communication is a critical aspect of living a positive life. Engaging in difficult conversations is one way to practice your communication skills. The more you face tricky topics head-on, the more practice you'll have at dealing with the hard stuff. This is not to say you should broach thorny topics unnecessarily, but don't shy away from them. You may benefit from those conversations more than you realize.

February 11

Remain open-minded when listening to others. Don't jump in with your comments too soon. Good listening skills are essential to positive relationships, but listening patiently doesn't always come easily. Resolve to give others your full attention when they are speaking. Do not allow your mind to wander to what you want to say next. Focus on the words (and body language) of those who are speaking.

February 12

Trust. Honesty. These are two essentials for creating positive relationships. Without them, the foundation of any relationship will be shattered. When you are trustworthy and honest, your interactions with others become a lot less complicated. You don't have to think about what you might say wrong. You don't have to worry about uncovering a secret or a dishonest statement. Never underestimate the power of trust or honesty.

February 13

If you want your ideas to be heard, you have to adapt to the communication styles of others. You must find ways to communicate your ideas so that others will understand them. To do this, you have to take the time to get to know the style of those you interact with. Do this by studying how they communicate their ideas to you. To be heard, it takes more than words alone.

February 14

An expression of gratitude, appreciation, or love can mean so much. The smallest token, the quickest compliment—even the littlest things can make a difference in another's day. Today tell one person how good she looks, how much you love him, how much she means to you. Love comes in so many shapes and sizes, but there's always enough of it to be shared freely and frequently with those closest to you.

February 15

No matter how much you might want to connect with someone, sometimes it can seem as though there are rivers and streams and entire oceans between you and another person. Weigh the pros and cons of that relationship. Is it worth the effort it takes to make that connection? Or is the connection you think you *want* something you don't necessarily *need*? Know that not every relationship should be pursued.

February 16

To cultivate a positive relationship, ask for feedback. Ask those you have close relationships with how you can improve your interactions with them. Sometimes a few small tweaks can have a hugely positive impact. Asking for feedback—and actually taking suggestions—isn't often painless, but being open to change and to new ideas enhances even the best of relationships.

February 17

It's always easy to look at others and say, "I can't connect with him or her because…" It's a lot more difficult to look at yourself and figure out what walls you might have up, walls that may be preventing you from having positive relationships. Put your hands out and feel for those walls. What's standing in your way? What do you have control over?

February 18

Pay attention to mood. By listening to the tone and speed of someone's voice while noting facial expressions and body language, you can get a good idea of what kind of mood someone is in. If you sense that someone is in negative state, consider giving him or her space—or asking how you can help. Also pay attention to your own mood when you interact with others; know when you are at your best—and when it might be best to be alone.

February 19

Relationships are often based on things you have in common with someone else. However, common interests aren't always positive. Often people bond over judging or putting down others. If you want to have a lasting, meaningful relationship, focus on positive common bonds that will bring you closer to another person. And be sure to check in on your relationships to make sure they remain based on positive, mutual interests and activities.

February 20

As people change and grow, relationships can become strained if one person (or both people) changes. If you want to maintain a relationship over a long period of time, you must be open to new experiences and perspectives. At his or her core, the person you are in a relationship with is the same. Strive to be open-minded when he or she seems to change—and encourage him or her to do the same for you should you change over the course of the relationship.

February 21

The whole "get what you give" concept is cliché, yes, but it's also true. If you want to be around a certain type of person, you need to *be* that type of person. If you don't feel you are the type of person you would want to spend time with, ask yourself, "What can I do to make myself the kind of person I want to spend time with?" When you think about what you want to see in others, you'll realize what you need to be yourself.

February 22

No one wants to be around someone who is negative. It's emotionally draining and mentally exhausting. One of the best ways to create healthy, enjoyable relationships with others is to be positive. People love being around people with positive energy, people who focus on the good things. Next time you're surrounded by others, take a moment to point out some positive things about the situation and see how others respond.

February 23

Learn to be interested in other people. For some, this can be tough, but the more interest you take in others, the more exciting interacting with them will be. When you learn to find other people fascinating, a world of possibilities opens up and almost any situation can become exciting. Even the most boring event can seem like an opportunity for optimism and insight.

February 24

You attract what you want to attract. The people in your life are there because they have been drawn to you in some way. If you don't like the people around you, you have to change yourself. If you want to attract positive people, you have to *be* positive. Become what you want to see in others and you will draw positive people to you the way the flame attracts the moth.

February 25

Your actions impact others. Choose wisely. Do not allow yourself to believe you are acting in isolation. Whatever you choose to do has an impact on many people—even when it might seem like it only matters to you. When making choices, consider others as well. When it comes to living a positive life, self-love is vital, but selfishness is lethal.

February 26

The right people will always bring you up, not down. They will always support you. They will never make you feel worthless or insignificant. If you have people in your life who make you feel bad about who you are, *get rid of them*. Life is too short to waste time on relationships fraught with negativity. Hard as it might be, let them go. You will be surprised by how quickly they are replaced by positive people.

February 27

Be grateful for the people in your life who support you. Finding and connecting with those who fill your life with light and love is not something you should ever take for granted. Say, "Thank you." Say, "I love you." Say the words that express just how lucky you feel to have positive relationships in your life.

February 28

Don't be afraid to open up your heart to new people. Love, friendship—they are so magnificent that they can be terrifying. Don't let the pain of the past hold you back from the possibilities of now. Embrace new relationships, new loves, with all you have. Dive right in and don't be afraid to get swept away. You will always find your way back to shore.

BONUS! February 29

Good relationships are like gravity. They bring you down to earth—and they are so stabilizing that they're often completely forgotten. Do not forget how valuable a good relationship is. Treasure it and make time for it. Pull yourself out of your work, your thoughts, and look around you. Ask yourself what relationships you've been taking for granted, what relationships could use a little extra TLC, and what relationships are no longer positive forces in your life.

GO BIG OR GO HOME

Inspiration

March 1

If you could have a dream come true, what would that dream be? Don't push your dream to the back of your mind, thinking *someday* . . . Don't deny the possibility that your dream could become a reality. If you want to live your most positive, most present life, you cannot deny your dreams. You cannot look at them like caged birds, something pretty behind bars. Instead, you must see them as something that should be set free.

March 2

Change the "I want" in your life to "I am." You cannot expect to get things you're not giving out. You cannot expect to make real the dreams you are not living. If you want something—kindness, strength, happiness, whatever—you have to *be* it. Every time you find yourself saying "I want..." remind yourself that you must instead focus on "I am..." You have to *be* instead of *want*.

March 3

You only have a limited amount of time in this life, and you should make the most of it. Spend your free time doing what makes you happy, what brings you closer to a dream-come-true. It's easy to get sucked into doing what other people want to do or justifying activities and saying that you "have" to do them, but do you really? Spend your time making your own dreams come true.

March 4

Don't look around at where you *think* you're going; instead, look where you *want to be* going. The things you focus on are the things you become. Think not about what you think *will* happen, but what you *want* to happen. Your thoughts have much more power over your life—and your attitude—than you realize. Choose those thoughts wisely.

March 5

You need to understand where you're going and why. You've chosen this path, but why? Why are you going in this direction? What does the path of your life look like? What's behind you? What's in front of you? Every day you make a choice to stay on this path. You could turn down another street or veer wildly into the grassy field beside the road. But you don't. Why? Understanding the path is very important to knowing who you are (and who you want to be).

March 6

Imagine you're standing in front of a fountain with a penny in your hand. In a moment, you will throw it in the water while throwing a wish out into the world. What do you wish for? If given one wish, one shot at going after anything, what would that desire consist of? On what would you use your one and only wish?

March 7

You deserve to have everything you want. You deserve the things you truly desire (even those things you tell no one about). Believe that and you will find ways to turn dreams into realities. Sometimes your dreams won't come true in the same way you imagined them, but if you go after what you want—and *believe* you deserve it—you will succeed.

March 8

What do you really, truly want from this life? If you listen to the voice inside you—the one that *really* knows what you want and isn't distracted by the doubts and fears created by the world outside your mind—you'll find out not what just what you want, but what you need. It's up to you to merge those wants and needs—to appreciate what you desire and acknowledge what's essential.

March 9

Let yourself enjoy a daydream today. Tucked inside the folds of that musing, you may find the inspiration you crave, the answers you seek. Dreams are the foundations for making things happen—as long as you remind yourself to come back to reality.

March 10

You know what? You got this. You might feel overwhelmed or discouraged at times, but you can do this. Whatever it is you want, you can have. Whatever it is you dream of, you can do. But you have to start off with the belief that you can. Today, tell yourself, "I got this. I can do this. I can make what I want a reality."

March 11

Believe you can achieve what you want—and, more importantly, believe you *deserve* to achieve it. If you cannot truly believe you deserve a dream-come-true life, imagine for a moment what it would be like if you *did* believe that. How would it feel to know you felt entitled to everything you ever wanted?

March 12

Not everything will fit together perfectly in life. There will be gaps and setbacks and missing pieces. That's okay. The mistakes and missing things will make you more conscious of what's there—and what *should* be there. Look for the empty spots in your life and think of how you would like to fill them. Then get to work patching things up and putting new things in place.

March 13

Stop doubting yourself. Stop believing that there might be a reason you cannot achieve what you want to achieve. You *can*. You *will*. But only if you rid your mind of doubt. Doubt, if you let it, will eat away at your inspiration until you are left with nothing. Do not allow that to happen. Push doubt aside and just go for it.

March 14

To be truly inspired, you must spark inspiration in others. To put your own dreams in motion, it helps to propel someone else's wishes. Inspiring others—either through a kind act, a thoughtful comment, or a grand gesture—will further inspire you as well. It is a win-win of inspiration and motivation.

March 15

You were born for this life. You were meant to do this—whatever it is you are doing. Keep at it. When it's hard, know deep down that it will get better. When it's impossible, find ways to stay inspired. You can seek inspiration outside yourself, but know that you will always connect with it most deeply when you uncover it within your heart and mind.

March 16

Do something today that scares you. Push yourself just a little bit further than you thought you could go. You, like all of us, tend to get settled into what you're used to. When you reach out and do something new—something a little bit scary—you'll find yourself inspired and invigorated. Everything that was once mundane will sparkle with just a little bit of magic.

March 17

Stop looking for four-leaf clovers. You must create your own luck. Believe you are lucky because you *are*. You have the power to make your own luck, to create your opportunities, to seek your own adventures. *That's* true luck. Don't waste time looking around for that rainbow and that pot of gold. Create your own rainbow, your own gold-filled pot of luck.

March 18

If it's meant to be, it will be. You have heard that saying before, but do you really believe it? You should. Have faith in the fact that things will work out how they should. The path might not always be clear, the end might not always be in sight, but someday it will all make sense. In the meantime, stay inspired. Stay focused on exploring the possibilities of everyday revelation.

March 19

Look closer at this life you're living. What matters most to you? If today were your last day, what would you want to spend it doing? And with whom would you want to spend it? What inspires you? Keep these thoughts in mind today as you go through your daily routine. Life is short. Life is too short to live uninspired.

March 20

Do not doubt the power of inspiration. It will keep you going when you feel you can no longer take one more step. It will soothe your heart when it's in need of mending. Inspiration is important— but it requires effort. Find one thing today that inspires you. Hold on to it in your mind, saving that image for a time when you will truly need your spirit to be rekindled.

March 21

Don't allow yourself to dwell in the shallows of over-thinking. Too much analysis holds you back; it stops you from diving in to whatever inspires and excites you. Give your life careful thought—but don't over do it. If you allow rumination to overtake you, you will always be standing on the sand while those truly inspired are diving enthusiastically into the waves.

March 22

The source of inspiration does not matter. Do not be swayed by what you think you "should" be inspired by. Inspiration can—and *does*—come from anywhere and everywhere. What inspires you might not inspire someone else. What everyone else finds inspiring might not spark inspiration in you. Accept that inspiration is unique and allow yourself to be inspired by whatever moves you.

March 23

Stop what you're doing and look around you. What do you see? What do you hear? What do you *feel*? There are so many things surrounding us that we take for granted, that we fail to be inspired by. In everything there is a bit of magic, a bit of sparkle that can enthuse you if you view it in the right light. Inspiration is *everywhere*. Look around.

March 24

There is that one song (or perhaps many songs) that moves you. You connect with its tune or lyrics in such a way that it feels as if you may have written it yourself. Listen to that song today. Remind yourself that there is something out there you can connect with in a deep and meaningful way. Embrace that feeling and keep an eye out for it in other aspects of your life.

March 25

Forget the notion that inspiration will hit you like a ton of bricks or a flash of lightning. It's rarely that way. Instead, inspiration usually creeps in slowly, through the back door, when you're not looking. It will sidle up next to you quietly and pull up a chair. It's not interested in grand entrances. Pay attention or you may miss its quiet arrival.

March 26

Inspiration is not opposed to routine. In fact, inspiration can become part of your day-to-day activities. You don't have to wait for inspiration to appear each day. You can *make* it happen by incorporating it into your life on a daily basis. Mark it on your calendar. Plan a date. Set aside time to be inspired.

March 27

Today is going to be a good day. You will find inspiration in an unexpected place. Let it soak into you like an unexpected downpour. Whatever inspires you today, let it flow. Don't hold yourself back or brush it off with excuses. Yes, there are always things to be done, items to be crossed off your to-do list. But there is only one today. Embrace the inspiration, whenever and wherever you find it.

March 28

Ask the right questions. Sometimes inspiration is not found in the answers, but in the questions. What questions are you asking yourself frequently? Are those truly the right questions, the ones you really want answers to? Today is not the time to worry about your answers. It is time to start reevaluating your questions.

March 29

What do you think when you first open your eyes every morning? Are you thrilled—or at least a little bit interested—by the prospects of the day? You should be. Each day has something to offer (even if you don't always recognize what that is until much later). If your initial thoughts each day aren't inspired, post a reminder to yourself on your phone or bedside wall to spark inspiration.

March 30

Inspiration doesn't come to those who are lazy. It requires work. If you want to be inspired, you have to *be inspiring*. Show others what you can do—what you can *be*—and you will find inspiration starts popping up all around you. To inspire others, you don't have to do anything crazy. Just be you. Everything you are should be inspiration enough.

March 31

They say March goes in like a lion and out like a lamb. Inspiration, too, goes in like a lion and out like a lamb. It is ferocious when you first encounter it—loud and bold and heart-pounding—but once it has settled within you, it is docile and bleats only occasionally for your attention. Even when it's no longer clamoring for your attention, don't ignore the things that once inspired you. You may have grown, moved away from them. They may have calmed, grown quieter. But they were once wild and thrilling ideas roaring with possibility. Revisit them from time to time. You might be surprised by what you find.

IT IS WHAT IT IS

Acceptance

April 1

Acceptance is the key to living a positive, present life. To live in the now, you must accept it as it is. You cannot wish it to be something else or create stories in your mind of how it should be. When you accept things for what they are, you worry less and feel more at peace. Acceptance is incredibly difficult—especially when things in life aren't going well—but learning to accept what is will make all the difference in living a positive life.

April 2

Strike these phrases from your vocabulary: "I wish," "I should have," "If only I had," and "It would be better if." These phrases serve no purpose other than to cause want and worry. You cannot go back and undo what has been done. You cannot waste time longing for what could be. You can only look around you right now and ask yourself, "What can do I do to make the most of this moment?"

April 3

It's okay to have a dream, a wish, a hope. It's okay to want things other than what you have right now. But it's not okay not to accept what's happening all around you. Because, like it or not, things are what they are. You can give them the labels of right or wrong, bad or good, but everything is what it is. A lack of acceptance leads to a lack of happiness.

April 4

Accepting others—and their actions—is part of acceptance. Not accepting others is a result of seeing the negative in them. Instead of focusing on why someone is different (or not what you want him or her to be), focus on what's good about that person and his or her choices and actions. Your way is not always the best way, and accepting others for what they are (and what they do) can lead you to new ways of seeing the world.

April 5

The world has not been painted in black and white. There are shades of gray in everything. Accepting what is allows you to see these shades, to know there is more than just one or two ways of seeing things. When you accept what is, you withhold your judgment. You observe the world around you with objective eyes. You allow it to be whatever color it needs to be.

April 6

A lack of acceptance can be a result of comparing things to the past. Do not think about what happened before and try to live accordingly; instead, focus on what's happening right *now* and live in response to this specific moment. Comparing things to the past always hinders an acceptance of what is. Do not let the things that have happened before get in the way of your quest for living positively in the present.

April 7

How does it feel not to be accepted? Not so great. Imagine that every time you choose not to accept what's happening, you are rejecting it, shunning it, making it feel bad. You have the power to bring moments—and people—to life, to fill them with acceptance and love. Don't deny yourself this power by choosing not to accept what is.

April 8

It's easy to abstractly think of yourself as an accepting person, but when it comes to your daily interactions, really pay attention to whether or not you are accepting others as they are. Are you *really* accepting them? Are you *really* not thinking your way of doing things is the best way? The only way to live a truly positive and present life is to accept what is, something you certainly can't do if you aren't accepting others for who they are.

April 9

Accept both the beautiful afternoon in which white clouds float lazily against a blue sky *and* the overcast mornings in which gray clouds hunch low from the heavy weight of the sky. They are same thing—clouds—but seen from a different point of view. Even while striving to live a positive life, recognize that there is value in accepting everything—even the negative things you encounter—because, like clouds, they may possess a beauty you have yet to see.

April 10

Do you accept where you are in your life? You might not like it—you might be longing for a change—but do you *accept* the position you're in? Even when you want change you must accept where you are. Where you right now are might not be exactly where you want to be, but refusing to accept it for what it is only hinders any progress you hope to make. Know that acceptance is not the same as settling.

April 11

When your mind is wandering constantly back to the past, you are not moving forward nor are you embracing the present moment. You are stuck in one spot, looking backwards. Remind yourself that the past—whether it was good or bad—is over. You cannot go back there and you will never again be the person you were in the past. You are you now. *Be* that person. *Love* that person. *Accept* that person.

April 12

Perfectionism holds you back from accepting what is. When you believe things, people, or you need to be perfect, you are refusing to accept those things or people for what they are. Ideas of "perfect" cause you to constantly search for something other than what is. Nothing is—nor ever will be—perfect. And that's why everything is so beautiful. Strive not for perfection, but for acceptance and life will appear more beautiful.

April 13

Do you honestly love your life—every little bit of it—as it is right now? Most of us would probably say no, we don't love *everything* about our lives. But why not? Why can't you love everything as it is right now? What's stopping you from accepting the idea that the life you're living right now is the best life and there is nothing better for you out there other than what you are experiencing right now? What would it be like to accept every little bit of your life for what it is?

April 14

The grass is not always greener. When you see what others have and desire those things or lifestyles, you're choosing to not accept what you have. You might think the lives or possessions of others hold more appeal than your own, but what should appeal most to you is the idea of accepting what you have, no matter what that is. In a place of acceptance, the grass is always greenest.

April 15

When you want things you don't have, you're struggling with acceptance. When you find yourself wanting, ask yourself: "Do I really want this? Why? Do I think it will make me happier? Why? Do I really need this in my life? Do I want this for the wrong reasons?" When you ask yourself these questions, you'll find that the desire for something new is actually a reflection of something missing within yourself, a hole you can fill by accepting who you are and what you have.

April 16

Imagine that your life is unfolding just as it should, that nothing is a mistake, and that everything is happening for a reason. What could you do, who would you be, if you truly believed that? What would life be like if you could fully accept it for what it is? Though the notion of relentless acceptance might seem as elusive as a dream, it's possible to accept—and love—your life, no matter what it consists of. It's all up to you and the outlook you choose.

April 17

You can cultivate acceptance in your own life by helping others to accept what they have. When you hear others complaining about what they want or don't have, remind them of all the things they *do* have. Remind them that, by not accepting life for what it is, they are only hurting themselves. Showing others the benefits of acceptance can remind you how powerful they are—and also remind you of all you have to be thankful for.

April 18

Acceptance doesn't mean keeping everything as it is forever. Acceptance can incorporate the idea of change. If there are things in your life you don't want to accept, change them and create an environment around you that is worthy of your acceptance. Change, in itself, can be a sort of acceptance, an active acknowledgment that accepting what is does not equal giving in—or giving up.

April 19

Accept what's given to you—especially when it comes to love. Accepting love can be a challenge. To accept it means you believe you deserve it, and you might not always feel worthy of love. Regardless of how you feel, you deserve every ounce of love you're given—and, more importantly, you are entitled to accept that love, to embrace it, and to say *yes!* to it.

April 20

It's hard not to compare and contrast others to who you are. And it's even harder not to be disappointed or unhappy when others don't live up to your expectations. But accepting others for who they are—not who we want them to be—is critical for positive relationships and for a positive life. Strive to understand others. Learning and knowing who they are on a deeper level will make accepting them much easier.

April 21

Accept the amount of time you have in your life. One great complaint of many people is, "I don't have enough time!" You do. You have the same amount of time as anyone else. Accept this fact— and accept the time given to you. It is yours to do with as you with, but don't waste it complaining. Complaints are direct refutes of acceptance. Stop complaining and use the time you are given wisely. Accept each moment and use it wisely.

April 22

While accepting what is, you must also pay attention what it is that you will not accept. Do not tolerate the things in life that drag you down. Do not settle for negativity. You have the ability to craft the life you want, and you should know that you deserve nothing but the best life. Acceptance is not about turning the other cheek. Acceptance is about knowing what is—and ridding your life of what isn't as it should be.

April 23

You do not always need to be in control. The more you accept what is, the less you will feel compelled to control your life and the lives of others. You will learn that life has a flow and you can go with it. When you allow yourself to simply *be*, to accept the moment for what it is, you will find yourself at peace—even if the moment you're experiencing doesn't seem very peaceful.

April 24

It takes a great deal of strength to accept what is. We are trained to want—and to want to change things. Change can be a wonderful thing, but a constant desire for things to be other than what they are leads to a lot of emotional anguish. Acceptance, just like positivity, takes practice. You will not find yourself embracing acceptance overnight. You must exercise your ability to accept. Every effort made will make you stronger.

April 25

When you find yourself stressed—wishing for a moment to be different from what it is—ask yourself, "Do I really have the power to change this situation right now?" If you do, take action and accept that you are making the most of the moment. If you don't, make the choice to accept the situation for what it is. In doing so, your restless mind will breathe a sigh of relief.

April 26

One reason people struggle to accept what is? Fear. They are afraid that they are missing out, that there is something better. Do not let fear stand in the way of accepting what is. This moment—and every moment that came before, and every moment that will come after—is worthy of acceptance. The moment you are in is the only moment that is real. If you choose not to accept it, you are choosing to avoid your own reality.

April 27

Perspective is important when it comes to acceptance. If you choose to look for the positive, you'll be more willing to accept whatever situation you're in. On the flipside, if you direct your attention toward negativity, acceptance will be harder to come by. Choose a positive perspective and accepting the world around you will come much more easily to you.

April 28

When striving for acceptance, start by stating the obvious. When you observe the world around you in factual statements (no adjectives or judgments needed!), you'll see that what you're facing isn't as difficult to accept as you might have thought. With plainly stated facts comes a sense of calm, a recognition that what's happening—disrobed from emotional phrases—is something you can easily accept.

April 29

The truth is, whether or not you choose to accept the moment for what it is, it's still going to be exactly that. Acceptance of something doesn't make it better or worse—it only impacts the way you relate to it and makes it more manageable (and enjoyable). Acceptance doesn't change what is—it only makes you more content with where you are, who you are, and what you're doing.

April 30

Accepting yourself is the jumping off point for accepting everything and everyone around you. When you are at peace with who *you* are, you can accept others for who *they* are. When you are in a place of acceptance, others don't challenge you. Situations don't threaten or trouble you. Accepting yourself is, perhaps, the hardest type of acceptance—but it is what lays the foundation for a positive and present life.

GIVE YOURSELF SOME LOVIN'

Self-Love

May 1

The best way to live a positive life in the present is to love who you are. When you love yourself—and truly accept who you are—everything changes. Everything in your life becomes a reflection of that love. You begin moving down the right path. You become surrounded by the right people. You are doing what you need to do, and you are making the most of every moment. This awesome feeling starts with the decision to fall in love with yourself.

May 2

If you want to love yourself, you have to have a positive mindset about every aspect of you—physical, mental, and emotional. You have to believe you're worthy of love, and you have to actively seek out positive things about yourself and your life. Change the way you think about yourself and the rest of your life will miraculously fall into place.

May 3

You are made up of many different attributes. You have a lot to offer to the world, just as you are. Do you really need that thing or person to make you more complete? Most of us have probably seen the film *Jerry Maguire* and heard the famous line, "You complete me." You know who should complete you? *You.* You should complete yourself. No matter how much you love or care about someone else, you are the only one who can be—and who can complete—you.

May 4

To fully love who you are, you must love who you have been. You must celebrate your past. This might be difficult (depending on what kind of past you have!), but remember: everything that happened to you in the past made you who you are today. Without the past—the good *and* the bad—you wouldn't be who you are now. So celebrate it, embrace it, *know* it. It is a part of you.

May 5

Not every desire should be indulged, but sometimes it's important to give in to the things that make you happy, that inspire you, that send little shivers of delight down your spine. Doing so will help you recognize the uniqueness that is you and will help you identify the things you should focus on more often—those things that truly bring you happiness.

May 6

It's okay to sing your own praises. In fact, you should do it often. When you do something wonderful or exciting, tell someone. Or, if that doesn't seem like something you're ready for, at least take a moment and acknowledge to yourself that you accomplished something really cool. Pause by the next mirror you see and tell yourself, "Remember that super cool/hard/amazing thing I just did? Damn. I *am* pretty awesome."

May 7

Do you ever find yourself ignoring your instincts or avoiding your gut reaction? Don't do that anymore. If you want to love yourself, you have to *believe* yourself. You have to trust yourself. It's not always easy to listen to yourself, but your thoughts and ideas are always valid (no matter how ridiculous they might seem). You don't always have to act on these thoughts, but always, *always* listen to them.

May 8

So there are some things you want to change about yourself, your body, your relationships, your life? That's okay. We all want to change things. But what if you stopped focusing on the things you want to change and, instead, focused on the things you want to stay the same? Appreciating all you have in your life is one of the very best ways to remember that you're lucky to be *you*.

May 9

The more you turn your attention toward yourself, toward the act of loving yourself, the more likely you will be to ask for more from life and to never, ever settle for less than you deserve. Loving yourself is about not settling for less than you deserve—and you deserve a lot. You deserve a lot from others—and you deserve every ounce of love you have to offer yourself.

May 10

Loving yourself goes hand in hand with knowing yourself. Who *are* you? What do you value? What do you love? What makes your heart start beating faster? What wakes you up panicked in the middle of the night? The more you know about yourself—the more you pay attention to your thoughts, choices, and actions—the more you'll be able to understand and love the person you are.

May 11

It is selfish not to have a good relationship with yourself because the relationship you have with yourself serves as the foundation for all other relationships. If you don't start out with a good foundation, all other relationships will face additional stress. Without loving, respecting, and accepting yourself, it's much more difficult (if not impossible) to love, respect, and accept others. *Love yourself first.*

May 12

Be open to receiving love—not only from others, but from yourself as well. Accepting your own love might be a challenge—often it's the hardest love to give and to receive—but know that doing so will improve all other aspects of your life. And, as a bonus, receiving your own love will positively impact the lives of those around you as well.

May 13

Accept yourself just as you are right now. Accept your flaws and your mistakes and your imperfections. Acknowledge those mistakes you've made, learn from them, and then forgive yourself for them. Recognize the ways you are flawed and then choose to accept and love yourself anyway. Not a single one of us is perfect and that's ok. Accept and forgive. And *love*.

May 14

Respect is an important aspect in any relationship, but it's essentially vital in the relationship you have with yourself. It's easy to *say* you respect yourself, but do you *really*? How do you treat yourself? Talk about yourself? Think about yourself? Make sure you are always respectful of yourself. You are valuable and important and you should always treat yourself as such.

May 15

Take a moment and think about the words you use to define yourself. Write them down. When you give it some thought, you may realize that you're creating a different version of you with your words. You are making yourself what you think you are (or, in some cases, what you think you should be). Now ask yourself: "Do I like the way I am defining myself? Are the positive and negative things I say about who I am really true?"

May 16

Make it a point to create a healthy environment for yourself. Care for your body. Surround yourself with positive people. Pay attention to your emotional and physical needs. A healthy environment is a way to show yourself love. It will support you and uplift you. It will be your safe place and your inspiration. Treat it as a sacred space and maintain it with kindness, love, and acceptance.

May 17

Don't waste time comparing yourself to others. You are amazing just as you are. You might struggle to believe that statement from time to time, but find a way to engrain these words in your mind: *I am amazing.* Others, too, are amazing. But there is only one you. There will only *ever* be one you. Don't waste time wanting to be what you're not when what you are is wonderful.

May 18

You are the best motivational tool you have. Other people might encourage you, but only *you* can really motivate you. Do whatever you have to do to remind yourself how great you are. Read books. Get off the couch. Talk to friends. Find ways to motivate your inner desire for self-love. Deep down you really want to love yourself, but sometimes you just need a little push in the right direction. And no one can give you a self-love shove quite like you can.

May 19

Question your perception. When you look at yourself in the mirror and cast judgment on yourself, ask yourself, "Is that *really* what's there or is that what I think I see?" When you're overly critical of yourself, ask yourself, "Is it *really* that bad or am I just looking at it that way?" Self-love is all about looking for the positive and focusing on what's great about you.

May 20

The words coming out of your mouth carry more weight than you might realize. Think about what you're saying. Are the words you use negative or positive? The more negative things you say about yourself—either out loud or in your head—the more you'll start really believing those words. Try saying, "Wow, I look great!" or "I feel amazing!" and see how those phrases make you feel.

May 21

People are more likely to focus on their failures than their achievements (probably as some sort of self-protection to avoid future failures). It's okay to acknowledge the things that didn't go so well, but if you really want to love yourself, you have to spend most of your time thinking about what you did or said right. Remind yourself: less scolding, more pats on the back.

May 22

Never forget that you are more than what you look like. Yes, it cannot be denied that physical appearance is important and has some merit, but it is not everything. The way society is set up makes it hard to remember this sometimes. Next time you look in the mirror and find your mind filled with negative thoughts, remind yourself that you are more than what is in that reflection. Your worth is more what you see in the mirror.

May 23

Love is limitless. It's not as if you have a ration of love and you have to dole it out carefully. You can love yourself as much as you want and still have plenty of love to give to others. That's the amazing thing about love; it's not something that comes in limited quantities. There is plenty of love in you to share both with yourself and others so don't hold back. Love yourself with all you've got.

May 24

Give yourself the luxury of downtime. You deserve to rest, to recuperate, to relax. Time for yourself is an essential part of self-love. Don't let anyone deny you this time. Moments of solitude will refresh you. Guard those moments fiercely—and believe you deserve them. Soak in the time you spend alone. Don't ever feel guilty for enjoying the pleasure of your own company.

May 25

Listen to yourself. When you get an idea, don't be the first one to shoot it down. Believe you can do it. Encourage yourself. Fill your mind with the belief that you can do *anything*, and you'll find that you can. When you hear negative voices whispering *you're not good enough* or *you can't do it*, silence them immediately. Listen to the real you— the one who believes you can do whatever you set your mind to.

May 26

Celebrate the little things about yourself. Look for the good traits, the stellar qualities, the well-executed decisions. You, and all your little victories, are worth celebrating. Each and every aspect of you has something positive within it. Embrace the little moments of joy, the aspects of yourself that often get ignored. Celebrate your one and only wildly wonderful life. Celebrate *you*.

May 27

Don't give up on yourself. You will have setbacks and disappoints. Life is like that. But don't give up on loving and believing in yourself. No matter what comes your way, you can handle it if you believe in yourself and love who you are. Love is a powerful force and directing it at yourself has positive and long-lasting consequences.

May 28

Loving yourself is a sort of salvation. When you love who you are, you become your own hero. You have powers beyond your imagination. You can save yourself from almost anything. Self-love serves as both shield and sword, protecting you from negativity and wielding positivity.

May 29

Know your boundaries. When you know what you will and won't accept in your life, you create a safe space of love for yourself. Don't tolerate others stepping over the boundaries you've created. To love yourself, you must protect yourself. And to protect yourself, you must know what you want—and, perhaps more importantly, what you *don't* want—in your life.

May 30

The more you value yourself and celebrate the good things about you, the more you'll want to celebrate the goodness in others. When you are constantly looking down on yourself or focusing on the negative, it can be difficult to find the positive in the world and in those around you. If you bring yourself up, you'll be much happier—and more likely to bring others up as well.

May 31

To truly love yourself, you must stop doing the things that make you unhappy. You must also stop interacting with negative people. The choices you make are reflections of how much you care about you. Choose to surround yourself with optimistic people. Choose to engage in constructive activities. Choose to create an uplifting life for yourself. It is the best way to show yourself love.

YOU'VE GOT THIS

Motivation

June 1

No matter what you want to do—you can do it. You just have to *believe* you can. You have to give it everything you have. Every moment is chance to do what you love, to be who you're meant to be. Don't waste another moment dwelling on what could have been or what could be. Now is the time to be what you want to be.

June 2

Are the people in your life positive influences? If so, they should be motivating you and inspiring you. Do you feel motivated by the people around you? Do they seem motivated in their own endeavors? Motivation, for the most part, is internal, but the people surrounding you can play a role in how motivated you are. Make sure you have the right kind of people around you—the kind who will urge you to keep going even when you feel like giving up.

June 3

You know that life is short, but do you really act like it's short? Between work or school, relationships, and commitments, you're only given so much free time to spend doing what you really love to be doing. Are you doing what you love during your precious hours of free time? Or are you doing what you think you should? Are you making the most of every minute? Because if you're not, you're wasting your time—and time is one of life's most valuable commodities. Be sure to spend it wisely!

June 4

Whether it's a bad book, a craft project, or an experience you've been trying to cross off your bucket list—if it's not making you happy, don't do it. We sometimes set goals for ourselves and feel we'll be let down if we don't achieve them. It's okay to admit something isn't what you thought it would be. It's okay to change your mind and realize you no longer want to do what you started doing. Changing your mind is okay.

June 5

Bust out of your comfort zone. Today is the day to abandon all fear, to break free of any barriers holding you back. If you had no fear, what would you do today? If you weren't restricted, what could you accomplish? Most of your roadblocks are in your own mind. Swerve around them. Break them down. Just *go*.

June 6

It's up to you to motivate yourself. Other people and outside influences can help, but you are the one who must push yourself in the right direction. You are the one who must choose your path and continue, day after day, to walk down it. You can be motivated by external factors, but the one thing that will always be there, that will always keep you moving forward, is *you*.

June 7

What do you need to stay on track with your goals? What do you need that you *already have*? Too often, we wait or delay because we think we need more than we do. What you already have is enough. With what you have, you can do so much more than you realize. Stop waiting for what you think you need. Start realizing that what you have is what is necessary.

June 8

On today's to-do list? Create a to-*don't* list. Make a list of things you *don't* want in your life. Craft a collection of all the things standing in your way. What can you get rid of immediately? What is weighing you down or holding you back? You can't make efficient progress if what you don't need in your life is dragging you down. Today is the day to let go of that extra weight. Leave the don'ts behind and focus on the do's.

June 9

The best way to motivate yourself is to get started. Even if it's a small step, get the ball rolling. Just as we're sometimes afraid of happiness, we're sometimes afraid to *do something*. Maybe you think you won't do a great job. Maybe you're frightened by what others might think. Maybe you're too uncertain about your own abilities. Whatever the excuse is, forget it! Rather than dwell on the negative aspects of what could happen, embrace the positivity of taking action.

June 10

Do you want things you're not going after? Do you wish for things but take no action to make them come true? It's time to stop wishing, stop waiting, and start *doing*. Today do one thing that will propel you in the direction of what you want. One thing can make all the difference between never-going-to-happen and I-can-do-this.

June 11

Even when you know you have to make something happen, sometimes you'll allow yourself to believe that you don't have the power to make it happen. You *do*. You have the power to make things happen. Choose not to slip into the shadow of powerless. Believe you can do it and you *will*.

June 12

Life isn't a fairytale. There is no handsome prince or fairy godmother. To get what you want, you must go after it. Waiting to be saved will only leave you wishing. You have the power to turn your wishes into realities, to check off your dreams with a satisfying, "Done!" If you want it done, you have to be the one to do it.

June 13

The time is never right. There is never a perfect moment to quit your job or leave a bad relationship or start your own business. There is never a perfect time to go after what you want, to become the person you want to be. The time is never right because it's *always* the right time. Now is right time.

June 14

Don't worry about what's in the future. Don't go digging around in the past. Stay in the now. Get to work, get started, right where you are. You don't have to worry about what could be or what has been. The only motivation you need is what's right now. Look around you. What you have now is what you once went after. Use this as motivation to keep going.

June 15

It's okay to grow frustrated when progress is slow, but don't let frustration stand in the way of making something amazing happen. Great things take time. Accept the pace (even when it's slow) and keep trudging along. Soon enough you will reach the crest of the hill and on the other side is a steep downward hill that will get the ball rolling with ease. Just keep climbing.

June 16

Push perfection aside. Perfect, as you may have heard, is the enemy of good. If you want to create a good life, you cannot aim for a perfect one. Motivate yourself not toward a place of perfection, but to a plateau of positivity. If you let the idea of perfection take root, you will stunt your own growth.

June 17

If you want to stay motivated, you need a plan. You need to know not only *what* you want, but also *how* you will get it. Take some time today to think about your plan. Think big picture and small details. Think about today and tomorrow and three years from now. With a plan in place, you'll be able to set expectations—and keep yourself motivated.

June 18

They might be tiny, but baby steps are powerful. Keeping yourself motivated can be as simple as doing one small thing every day to move you in the direction of getting what you want. Don't underestimate the power of little victories. Every little thing that moves you toward your goal is an accomplishment. Be proud of those baby steps.

June 19

A shift in perspective can be just what you need to stay motivated. Try to see what you want from a different point of view. What would it look like to someone else? What would it look like to the younger you? The older you? A fresh point of view can brighten your motivation like a fresh coat of paint, making it seem brand new again.

June 20

Imagine the best possible scenario. What if you actually got what you're going after? Use that image as motivation to keep going. If possible, create a visual representation of that image and place it somewhere you will see it often. The more you focus on positive outcomes, the more motivated you'll be to keep going when the going gets tough.

June 21

Open-mindedness is crucial to motivation. The more open you are to new ideas and fresh perspectives, the more likely you'll be to stay on track. You'll feel a renewed sense of excitement when you look at your goals from a different point of view. Having trouble finding new ideas to open your mind? Ask others what motivates them and consider how to apply those ideas to your life.

June 22

Motivation requires a narrow focus. It's tempting to try to do everything and anything associated with what you love, but if you do *everything*, you'll find yourself overwhelmed and not doing much of *anything*. So start small. Figure out what you're most interested in—one aspect of what you love most about life—and zero in on that.

June 23

A positive attitude can work wonders when it comes to staying motivated. Whenever you find yourself losing hope or questioning your progress, contemplate all you've already done—and all you plan to do. Don't allow yourself to dwell under a cloud of negativity. Instead, look for the blue skies, the golden sun, the possibility that you *will*, in fact, make your dreams come true.

June 24

It's never too late to start—or to start over. Sometimes your goals or dreams won't turn out exactly the way you thought they would, but that's okay. It's okay to admit things aren't going as you planned—or maybe they are and you're just not so sure about the plan anymore. It's okay to take your motivation and redirect it.

June 25

Inspiration can be a foundation for motivation. The two terms are separate but intertwined. Use what inspires you to stay motivated. Take the emotions you feel when you're inspired and use those emotions to guide yourself down the path that's best for you. Seeking new, fresh inspiration will also renew your motivation.

June 26

Ask yourself, "What am I motivated by?" Motivation can come in many forms—and not all of them positive. Are you motivated by money, fear, or greed? Are you motivated by anger, pain, or worry? These are not good motivations. Make your motivations positive. Become motivated by hope, love, and progress. Become motivated by curiosity, excitement, and happiness.

June 27

Stop allowing yourself to default to "someday." Waiting is a risk. There might not be a someday. There might not be a tomorrow. Clouded in negativity as that might sound, the truth of living now shines through like a silver lining. If there is something you're dreaming of, don't wait for it. Do it now. If you don't, you could end up looking back at a lifetime of days you simply said, "Someday…"

June 28

To find what truly motivates you, learn to read the whole story. When looking for motivation, we often look right around us. But your life is bigger than that. You might think you're looking in the right places, but as a character in your own story, you're so close to the action that there's a lot you might be missing. Take a step back and read the big picture.

June 29

Would you rather work tirelessly for the life you want or settle effortlessly for a life you don't want? There's no magic wand to transform what it is into what you want it to be. It's going to take a lot of hard work, but if you really want it, you'll be much happier making moves than wasting time. You'll be much better off working than waiting.

June 30

Make motivation part of your daily routine. You need a daily dose of it to keep yourself focused on what you want. Create a habit that helps you to stay motivated. Or keep motivational words or images nearby so you don't lose sight of your dreams and goals. In the day-to-day hustle, motivation can get lost. Find a way to make sure you'll always find it.

GET IT TOGETHER

Productivity

July 1

The foundations for positive productivity are: organization, motivation, inspiration, and preparation. Without these four things, producing results of any kind will be a challenge. You must learn to motivate and inspire yourself. And, perhaps even more challenging, you must learn to prepare and organize. With these four productivity must-haves in hand, you will be unstoppable.

July 2

Today is the day you master the art of the to-do list. First and foremost: create the list in a convenient place. Whether it's on your phone, on your computer, or on a piece of paper, choose a place that's easy to access. Next, get a system in place. Put daily to-dos on a list; put monthly tasks on a calendar. Use a system that works for you. Finally, actually *use* the lists you create—and edit any part of the list-making system that's not working for you.

July 3

Every item in your home/office/etc. should have a place—and you should know exactly where that place is. Each time you use an item, put it back in its designated place. Doing so will save you time (and help you avoid stress!) the next time you're looking for that item.

July 4

Don't be afraid of delegation. Even if you like to be in control, one way to keep things productive is to delegate tasks to others. No matter how skilled you are you can't do *everything*. And you'll be surprised how many people will be happy to help. If you aren't up for a task—or don't think you can do it well—delegate. Delegation can be a productivity lifesaver.

July 5

Putting things off is a great way to create stress and feel unproductive. Don't procrastinate today. If you can do it today, *do it*. "I don't feel like it," is not an excuse. Do what you can today because you never know what tomorrow will bring. You don't want to look back and say, "I wish I'd done that yesterday!"

July 6

You don't need fancy organizing bins or carefully selected day planners to be productive. You can use what you have and make it work for you. Everything around you has the ability to be put in order, to be organized to suit your needs. Don't make excuses by saying you don't have the right tools or equipment. What you think you need, you don't. What you truly need, you have.

July 7

Learn to say "no." If someone asks for your help and you don't have the time or energy, be honest and admit you can't offer your assistance at the moment. It can be hard to turn requests down (especially from those close to you), but the more you pile on your plate, the less productive you'll be—and the more stressed out you'll become.

July 8

Every so often, you'll come up against some productivity resistance. Something, someone, or even yourself will stand in the way of you and doing something productive. Occasionally give in to those bouts of unproductivity. Let yourself relax and be in the moment—even if you have a million more "productive" things to do. Remind yourself that being here and now is, in itself, productive.

July 9

Watch out for self-sabotage, for those moments you tell yourself that you're being productive even when you know that's just not true. Don't allow for the rationalization of laziness. Relaxation is imperative for living a positive life; laziness is not. Ask yourself, "Am I being lazy or am I just relaxing?" When you relax, you're taking a break. When you're lazy, you're missing out on potential breakthroughs.

July 10

Productivity starts with preparedness. You have to be ready to tackle each and every day. Nothing gets you ready like a game plan. Create a to-do list. Lay out your outfit the night before. Pack your lunch ahead of time. Do the little things now so you can triumph over the big things later.

July 11

Go through your possessions (and I do mean *all* of them) and get rid of the things you don't need or want. Give it away if you can. If you can't, throw it away. You *can* do it. Don't waste another second. Don't weigh the pros and cons of keeping it or not. If you don't need it, don't use it, and don't love it, get rid of it. All the things you have but don't need stand in the way of productivity.

July 12

Color-coding has its benefits. So do labels and lists and filing cabinets. Take advantage of the organizing tools you have at your disposal (some of which are on your computer and are free!). If you don't know where to start when it comes to organizing, do a little online search. You'll find endless amounts of resources. The more order you create in your life, the less time you'll waste, and the more productive you'll be.

July 13

Contemplate the clutter standing between you and a positive, productive life. What is blocking you emotionally? What physical elements are standing in your way? To be productive (and positive!), you must clear away the clutter—emotional, physical, etc. In doing so, you'll find a clarity that leads to an abundance of productivity.

July 14

Take a moment to consider all the productive things you've done over the past few days. So often, we focus on all that we have to do that we don't consider all that we've already done. Productivity flourishes with a few pats on the back. Remember to periodically remind yourself of all you've accomplished.

July 15

Trust yourself. When you trust yourself, you believe you have the ability to cross those items off your to-do list. You believe you can conquer any task. Have faith in your ability to be productive. And don't forget—just because you might struggle with productivity from time to time doesn't mean you're not making progress.

July 16

Assess the pros and cons of your actions. What might *feel* productive might not actually be. Make sure you know not only what you're doing, but also *why* you're doing it. Don't let yourself get settled in your routines (no matter how productive they seem!) simply because they appear to be working. Always stay open to new ways of doing things. Always be ready to reevaluate what's working and what's not.

July 17

Do not have a junk drawer/box/room. *Ever.* Junk drawers (and rooms and closets...) are bottomless pits of disorganization. They encourage you to be disorganized by allowing you to have a place to put the things you don't know what to do with. If you come across something that doesn't have a place, create a place for it. If you don't want to create a place for it, it's junk. Everything should have a place, and things that don't have a place should find a place in the garbage can or the recycling bin.

July 18

Accountability aids immensely in productivity. Find someone who will help you stay on task. Ask someone to check in with you on a weekly or monthly basis to see how much progress you've made. You and only you can be truly responsible for your productivity, but it helps to have someone giving you a little nudge every now and then.

July 19

Stop multi-tasking. It might feel like it's making you more productive, but studies have shown that it diminishes your productivity levels. Instead of tackling everything at once, set aside time for each task you need to accomplish. One thing at a time can add up to lots and lots of productivity.

July 20

Find yourself feeling distracted? In today's world, it's no wonder. There are so many ways to lose your focus. For this reason, you have to create a place of productivity, to cultivate a culture of can-do. If you want to get it done, create a distraction-free environment for yourself. This might mean switching things up—but sometimes that change is just what you need to get going.

July 21

It's time to take a break. Productivity happens when you make time for relaxation. What makes you feel at peace? What creates a sense of calm? Make sure to incorporate mini-breaks into your day. And make sure those breaks are truly breaks—don't just swap one to-do for another. Take a walk. Take a drive. Call a friend. Separate yourself, just for a little while, from that to-do list.

July 22

What are your priorities? Are you spending time on the things that *really* matter to you? Sometimes productivity is aimed in the wrong direction. Make sure the hours and days you spend being productive are focused on the things you desire. Don't be productive doing what you "should" do. Use your productivity for the life you want, the life you deserve.

July 23

Complications are part of life, but not all complications are out of your control. What complicates your life? What complications stand between you and being productive? Can you get rid of any of these? Be honest about what you actually have control over. You may have more power than you realize.

July 24

Productivity requires energy—and it's up to you to keep yourself energized. When you feel tired and drained, take a walk, eat a healthy meal, or pause for a rest. Don't push yourself harder than you need to be pushed. Energy is essential. If you push yourself too hard, you'll drain yourself of that very valuable resource.

July 25

Are you doing what you love to do? If you are, being productive will come effortlessly. You'll *want* to do all the things on your to-do list. If you don't love what you're doing, productivity will be a constant struggle. Figure out what you're passionate about and go after it. Living a life you love makes productivity pleasurable.

July 26

Today is No More Excuses Day. It's time to drop whatever excuses you've been using to put off productivity—too tired, too busy, too stressed— and simply get to work. No more excuses. No more reasons why you can't do what you really want to do. The only thing standing in your way is you. Break through your own excuses and you'll find what you want deep down: progress.

July 27

People who drag you down emotionally will suck the life out of your productivity. Are there people in your life who bring you down? Are there people who weight you down with their negativity? It's time to rid your life of those people. Or, at the very least, limit your interactions with them. If you want to be productive, surround yourself with positivity—and productivity.

July 28

How seriously do you take sleep? If you're looking for a high level of productivity, you better take it pretty seriously. Do some experimenting to find out how many hours of sleep make you feel amazing. Strive to achieve that perfect sleep-wake balance as often as you can. Rest can work wonders in all aspects of your life, but it's almost magical what a good night's sleep can do for your productivity level.

July 29

Look around you. Is what you see the sign of a productive environment? If the space around you is messy or disorganized, your progress may be hindered. Strive to keep a clean, organized area for ultimate productivity. Order and organization can go a long way to making your dreams come true.

July 30

For one hour today, turn off your phone. Click out of your email. Take a break from all technology and *focus*. Direct your attention to whatever task ranks highest on your to-do list. Prepare for any potential distractions and avoid things that will keep you from getting done what you need to do. It sounds difficult—turning off technology—but once you get into the groove, you'll be so pleased with your progress.

July 31

Fear can impact how productive you are. You might be afraid of actually getting what you want, which puts a blockade between where you are and taking action to getting where you want to be. Don't let the fear of making things happen hold you back. Stay motivated, inspired, organized, and prepared and productivity will seem a lot less intimidating.

EYE OF THE BEHOLDER

Beauty

August 1

Beauty might be in the eye of the beholder, but the beholder will only see it if she has her eyes open. Are you looking for the beauty in your life? It's there, all around you. It's *everywhere*. It's in your daily routines. It's in the unexpected celebrations. It's in every season, every morning, and every night. Beauty isn't always what you think it should be. It's whatever moves you, whatever makes you smile. The trick is not just to simply *see* beauty, but to actively *look* for it.

August 2

Why look for beauty in everything? Because beauty makes life better. Just think about how you feel when you see something beautiful. You are in awe. You are moved. You are excited. Now imagine what it would be like to feel that way all the time. What if you could see the beauty in everything? What if you could be excited by the gorgeousness in every person, place, and thing you come across?

August 3

When you're looking around for all the beauty in this wild, crazy life, keep an open mind. You'll miss out on a lot of beauty if you're focused on the ideal or typical standards of beauty. Beauty is so much more than what society often limits it to. Try looking at things from a fresh point of view and all the beauty you'll find will amaze you.

August 4

Beauty is boundless. You have no limit to the number of times you can say, "You're beautiful" or "That's beautiful." So say it. Think it. *Believe* it. Beauty, in all its many forms, can inspire you. Soak up that inspiration. And pass it on. Point out the beautiful things you see. Tell those you love how beautiful they are. Spread the word about all the beauty in this world.

August 5

There is beauty in believing. There is beauty in believing in yourself, in things beyond your control, in that which you cannot understand. Believing in all that you are—and all that you can be and do—is a beautiful thing. Celebrate what you believe in. Bask in the beauty of believing.

August 6

Draw back the shades. Open the window. Let the beauty of the outside come inside. Let the light shine in and the air circulate through. No matter what the weather, throw open the windows today and celebrate the beauty of the outdoors allowed in. Consider what other types of beauty you might let in if you only opened up your windows.

August 7

Beauty often gets forgotten when you do the same thing over and over again. In the middle of a common routine, pause and ponder what is beautiful about that moment. The things you do most often, over and over again, often hold unexpected beauty.

August 8

Use your five senses to find beauty all around you. What do you see? Hear? Feel? Taste? Smell? Beauty comes in so many different forms, though we so often think of it as visual. Today pay attention to all of your senses in your quest for beauty. Surprise yourself with the beauty you can find when you look, touch, taste, smell, and listen.

August 9

Do you see beauty when you look in the mirror? You should. Everything about you—even the parts you don't love—is beautiful. Don't let anyone (or society) tell you anything different. You are beautiful just as you are. Every piece of you fits together just as it should. Make a point to look at yourself today and remind your reflection: "I am beautiful."

August 10

There is beauty in pushing yourself outside of your comfort zone. Try something new today. When you do, pay attention to how it makes you feel. Note the thrill that comes with doing what you don't usually do. Note the beauty that can be found in the exhilaration of something new. Strive to be open to new experiences, to embrace the beauty of excitement.

August 11

Even sadness possesses beauty. There is beauty even in the hardest times. Rather than rejecting negative emotions, embrace and explore them. Look for the beauty in feeling something—even if it is sadness or anger or irritation. Emotions, no matter what they are, are beautiful. Dwell on the positive ones, but don't avoid the negative. Those possess beauty too.

August 12

Do not allow others to steal beauty from you with their negative comments or actions. Choose to think for yourself—to view life through your own picturesque lens. When you find the beauty in something, don't allow that beauty to be refuted. Let others think what they want about beauty, but don't allow them to steal what you believe is beautiful from you.

August 13

How do you define beauty? Ask yourself what you consider to be beautiful and why—and then dig deeper. Is there a way to create more beauty in your life by expanding that definition of beauty? Have you restricted yourself by believing in a limited definition of what is beautiful? If so, consider how you can expand how you define beauty to include so much more. Remember: beauty is *everywhere* and in *everything*.

August 14

When it comes to physical beauty, most cultures celebrate symmetry. The more symmetrical a person's facial features are, the more he or she is considered beautiful. But what about asymmetry? Asymmetrical differences can be just as beautiful as symmetrical similarities. Today find something that is asymmetrical—and celebrate its beauty.

August 15

Look around you today and identify the five most beautiful things you can see. (These can be people, items, experiences—anything you think is beautiful.) Spend a few minutes thinking about those things today. Contemplate why you enjoy them and why you find them beautiful. Then consider how you might incorporate more of these beautiful things in your life.

August 16

Beauty—and the identification of it—is unique. What you find beautiful, others might not. It's okay to have differing opinions when it comes to beauty. In fact, it's a wonderful thing that two people can have completely distinct ideas of what is beautiful. There is beauty in opinions—and there's even more beauty in accepting what others find beautiful. Even if you don't see beauty right away, keep an open mind. You never know when your perspective might shift.

August 17

Confucius said, "Everything has beauty, but not everyone sees it." Do you see beauty today? Are you open to it? When things are difficult, it will be a struggle to find the beauty. You must stay open to it. You must look for it. Sometimes you have to get your hands dirty. Sometimes you have to dig a little deeper to find beauty beneath the surface.

August 18

Love is beautiful. It is one of the most beautiful things there is. Celebrate the love in your life, the love of your life. Celebrate all the love you've experienced—and all the love you will experience in the future. Look at the ones you love and remind yourself of all the beauty you see in them. Beautiful are those who love—but those who celebrate love are drop-dead gorgeous.

August 19

The act of making someone else feel beautiful is one of the most beautiful things in the world. Today go out of your way to make someone else shine, to highlight his or her strengths. Even a simple compliment can make someone's day or turn an ugly moment into a lovely one. Spread beauty wherever you go today.

August 20

Some of the most beautiful people have gone through tough times. They have struggled and come out stronger. Their strength makes them even more beautiful. Every tragedy, every scar, makes you more beautiful. Each heartache, each tear, makes you lovelier. Remember this the next time you find yourself suffering. The pain you feel is a gateway to strength. The strength will make you even more beautiful than you already are.

August 21

There is one and only you. How beautiful is that?
To know you are the only you that will ever exist
is a truly beautiful thing. Celebrate your you-ness.
Remind yourself of all the beauty that's been
brought into the world simply because you are
here. Your beauty is invaluable. *You* are priceless.

August 22

Beauty should not be caged or chained. It should
be allowed to change and shift. Free your mind to
the idea that beauty can take different shapes.
Time will change what you think is beautiful—or
how you think it's beautiful. Let beauty do its thing.
Let the beautiful things in your life become what
they need to become. Accept then for what they
were, what they are, and what they will be.

August 23

Today—like everyday—is the most beautiful of days. Wake yourself with a smile. Go to sleep with a grin. And in between those moments when your head rests on your pillow, celebrate every delicious minute of this day. It will only happen once. Capture its beauty while it lasts.

August 24

Beauty cannot always be put into words or explained clearly. Don't waste time trying to fit beauty into a box, to label it. Accept it for what it is. Words may not do it justice, but the way you feel about something beautiful will serve it well. Allow yourself to go without words, to spend time soaking up the beauty around you without trying to define it.

August 25

At times beauty can seem like excess. But we need it. It inspires us. It thrills us. Don't discount the power of beauty in your own life. It's a form of sustenance. Beauty feeds your soul. It is delicious and delectable. Dig in. Gobble it up. Don't be afraid to go back for seconds.

August 26

What's real is beautiful. Look around at this moment. What's happening right now is where beauty lies. Beauty exists not in the past or the future. It is in the now. You may want to recall the beauty you've seen or pine for the beauty you've yet to see. But, instead, focus on the beauty of this moment. Zero in on the beauty of *now*.

August 27

Beauty doesn't have to have a purpose. Beauty can be just for its own sake. If you must find a reason to seek beauty, remind yourself that the act of looking for the good in life is reason enough. The smile something beautiful brings to your face, the moment you inhale sharply when you spot something beautiful, and the joy that comes with creating beauty are, in themselves, filled with dazzling intention.

August 28

Sometimes beauty comes in the absence of something else. The absence of noise can be beautiful. So can the absence of pain or regret. Look around for negative feelings, situations, or people that are currently missing from your life and observe the beauty of their absence. Note how beautiful it feels to be without the things that bring you down.

August 29

Beauty comes when you get not what you want, but what you *need*. What do you have in your life that you need? What fulfills you? What could you not live without? Today rejoice in the needs that are met, the beauty that comes with having what you need (even if you're without everything you want). Recognizing needs met is a beautiful thing. Gratitude is gorgeous.

August 30

A great deal of beauty lies within you. Close your eyes and look within. Search for the beauty that's not visible to the naked eye. There is beauty in your courage, your strength, and your heart. There is beauty in your thoughts, your emotions, and your soul. Close your eyes and you will see it.

August 31

Beauty is not only something you can observe. It is something you can create as well. If you want a beautiful life, you must create one. You bring beauty into your life with the words you speak, the thoughts you think, and the actions you take. Everything you do can be beautiful. Attract beauty by *being* beautiful.

SEPTEMBER

SHAKE THINGS UP

Change

September 1

Change—both expected and unexpected—can be challenging. It shakes things up—but this shake-up can be a good thing. Change provides a fresh perspective. It makes you look up and pay attention. What you see when faced with change has a lot to do with the perspective you choose. Whenever change comes your way, seek to see the good. Look for all the benefits that come along with shaking things up.

September 2

Is it always darkest before the dawn? Sometimes change comes not when you expect it, or not in the ways you would expect it. It's not always a burst of sunlight on the horizon, casting light over everything. Change is often slow and steady, happening over time until one day you wake up, look around, and realize everything is different.

September 3

Unexpected change can be frustrating. But it can also be eye-opening and inspiring. It's all a matter of how you choose to look at it. It's easy to focus on the negative when things unexpectedly don't go your way, but the next time you're faced with an unanticipated change ask yourself, "Do I want to love this change or hate it?" One option might be easier, but consider trying to embrace the option that will make your life more positive.

September 4

Every change is a chance to learn. If you want to make the most of changes, look for the lessons in them. Each and every change comes with a nugget of wisdom. Those great life lessons might not always be easy to spot, but if you look closely, you will see them—those sparkling bits of gold among the dirt.

September 5

Coping with change may be complicated. Don't feel as if you have to deal with it on your own. Ask for help. Spend time with positive people. Reach out to others. No matter what type of change comes your way, you can gain a lot from seeking support. You can cope on your own, but having supportive people around you can help you handle change.

September 6

Loss can be a part of change. Dealing with loss positively can be difficult—but it is not impossible. Start by allowing yourself to feel. It's okay to be sad or heartbroken. Accept your emotions. Change often brings a flood of emotions—both positive and negative. Don't push your feelings aside. Instead, embrace them and allow yourself to feel what you need to feel.

September 7

Whether you love or loath change, you'll be forced to face it at some point. How you deal with it is all up to you. You have the power to interpret change in your own way. And, more importantly, you have the power to interpret change *positively*. Change is inevitable. Your attitude toward it is malleable.

September 8

Accept the change in your life for what it is. Try to look at the situation objectively. Ask yourself, "What's *really* going on here?" Strive to accept the facts—and the emotions that come along with them. Resisting what is—emotionally or otherwise—won't do any good. It only creates more pain and distress in your life. Keep in mind that the only thing a lack of acceptance will do is make a situation harder.

September 9

Describe the change you're facing. But here's the catch—only describe the good things. Ask yourself, "What is good about this situation?" Think of the positive aspects this change will bring you. Even if a situation seems horrible, there are good things you can focus on. Look closely at what's changed and ask, "What's positive about it? What can I learn from this change? What can it teach me about myself?"

September 10

With change often comes comparison. Don't look back to what was and wish it could be that way again. Don't look to the future and wish things could someday be different. Take a step back from comparison and accept the moment—and all the changes you face—for what it is. Stay present. In doing so, accepting change will come much more easily to you.

September 11

Even when you can't see it, change is making you stronger. It might feel like its knocking you down to the ground, trampling all over you, but every time change comes your way, it's actually building you up and making you better. Even when it's tough, stay focused on the strength you're building. Remind yourself of how strong you are—and how much stronger you will become.

September 12

Change doesn't always just happen. Sometimes we have to *make* it happen. What could use some changing in your life? Settling for the way things are is a mistake. You should always be open to change; you should always be looking for ways to improve your life. Today is the day to evaluate the things in your life that could use some tweaking. What could be better? What could you do differently? Look for the little changes you can make instantly. Often these little changes have the biggest impacts.

September 13

If you can, anticipate change and try to plan for it. Anticipating change isn't always possible, but if you can do it, you'll be more prepared. One way to be aware of change coming your way? Try to be in tune with the world around you. Pay attention to what's going on in the lives of those close to you. Look at your environment and your relationships. The more in tune you are with your world, the less likely change will sneak up on you unexpectedly.

September 14

You cannot control everything (no matter how much you might want to!). Choose to accept what you cannot change, as well as the changes that are out of your control. Accepting what you cannot control will soothe you; it will provide you with a sense of peace that cannot be found when you resist what you cannot change.

September 15

People change. Over time you will change. Over time the people you love will change. Learn to adapt to the changes of others. Don't hold it against them when they make modifications to who they are. Change is part of the human experience, and if you resist it, you be left standing in stagnant waters.

September 16

It takes courage to willingly choose to change. It can be terrifying, the thought of changing your life, of changing yourself. But don't let fear hold you back if you know something in your life needs to change. You have to take whatever fear you're experiencing and just let it go. This is *not* easy— but it is the only way to really prepare for a change you know needs to be made.

September 17

When you feel yourself changing, listen to how that feels. Ask yourself what's made you change—and if that change really is for the better. Get an unbiased opinion if you can. Change can be a wonderful thing, but it can also be dangerous. Make sure the changes you make in your life are positive changes.

September 18

Without change, life would grow stale. Everything we do—everything we are—would begin to bore us. Remember that the next time you face a difficult change. Without change, you wouldn't be growing. And without growth, you cannot live a truly positive life. Change (even with all its challenges) brings an element of excitement to life. Celebrate that thrill.

September 19

Change can be so brutal sometimes. It's hard to face it when it's forced on you, but it's even more difficult when you're trying to implement it yourself. At that point, change becomes a choice and, for that reason, it's something you can so easily avoid or give up on. Make sure you're ready to change. If you're not ready, you won't stick with it. But if you're ready and willing to put in the effort, you have the amazing ability to turn your whole life upside down (or right side up!).

September 20

It's never too late, you're never too old (or young!), to change. Even if change seems beyond your wildest dreams, it is always attainable. But it takes work. Change doesn't happen overnight. If you want something in your life to change, you have to *make* it change. Step out of your comfort zone. Cast aside your fear. *Go for it.*

September 21

If there are things in your life you cannot change, know that you can always change the way you think about them. Change is not always within your control, but the way you see the world is. What can you do to change your perspective today? How can you look at the things in your life that you'd like to change but cannot and see them in a positive light?

September 22

All change is not necessarily positive. Sometimes we make changes in our lives that make things harder. Sometimes we choose to do what we know isn't right for us. Next time you make a choice or choose to change, ask yourself, "Will this change bring more positivity into my life? Will changing in this way bring me closer to the person I want to be?" Do not be pressured by changes you "should" make. Do what's right for you.

September 23

Deep down there is a part of you that will never change. There is a part of you that remains consistent throughout your entire life. When you're struggling with change, try to reconnect to that ever-present part of yourself—your *muchness*. This is the essence of who you are; connecting with it will help you cope with change.

September 24

With change often comes stress. When change comes your way, make a point to take a time out. Whether it's a deep breath or a walk around the block (or, hey, even a spa vacation!), take a break from whatever's going on in your life, from the change, and give yourself a chance to relax. Being stressed will never help you cope with a situation. If you can find a place of peace—even one within your own mind—change will seem less daunting.

September 25

Look for the silver lining amid the clouds of change. In every change, there is something beautiful, something of value. It may be gift of inner strength. It may be a source of inspiration. Change, in all its many forms, has much to offer you if you are willing to look past the clouds. Don't be so set on finding some golden nugget of truth that you miss change's silver lining.

September 26

You know what complaining about change gets you? *Nothing.* Grumbling and whining does no good when it comes to coping with change. Sure, a quick vent to a friend or relative can help ease your mind, but don't harp on the negative aspects of change. If there's something you can do about it, do it. If not, stop wasting time whining and start striving to make the best of the situation.

September 27

Being flexible makes it much easier to deal with change. Imagine yourself as an unbreakable rubber band. Sometimes change will stretch you to the point when you think you might break, but if you just hold on, you will bounce back again.

September 28

When you're struggling with change, find ways to incorporate the familiar. Spend time with people close to you. Keep items near by that make you feel happy and relaxed. Intertwine the new with the old, the recognizable with the unknown. Even having one familiar item or person by your side can make any transition easier.

September 29

Staying present is the best way to make the most of change. Being mindful of the moment helps you focus on what is happening right now—rather than what has already happened or what might happen in the future. If you can get through this one moment (and you can!), you can get through anything. Take change one moment at a time.

September 30

Psych yourself up for change. Running from it might seem more like what you want to do, but don't. Get into it. Get excited for it. Even when it seems less-than-ideal, you never know what surprises a new change will bring. You never know what lies around the next corner.

IT'S NOW OR NEVER

Mindfulness

October 1

October, and all of the changes it brings to the world, serves as a reminder that we too are changing. We, like the leaves in the autumn trees, are fading, our colors transforming without warning. October is an annual reminder of your mortality, a reminder to live each day more fully, more mindfully.

October 2

The more you worry and stress about the future, the less likely you'll be to enjoy the present moment (the only thing that's truly guaranteed). If you're not living in the present, you're not really living. Stay in the now as much as you can. Don't look to the future as a place where you will someday be happier or wealthier or better. Now is the place where you are perfectly you.

October 3

If you're struggling to be mindful, ask yourself, "What's awesome about this moment?" In every moment, there is something awesome. Look at the details. Take into account the big picture. In every moment there is awesomeness—if only you direct your attention to it. Make an effort to pinpoint the awesome found in this very moment.

October 4

Just being alive is pretty amazing. How often we take it for granted! Focus today on how wonderful it is to be here—to be a living, breathing you. Consider all the things about your life that are remarkable. One of the most amazing things is your ability to breathe. Breathing is such an unconscious act that we often take it for granted. Take a few deep breaths today and center yourself in the moment.

October 5

How would you describe this moment to someone? When struggling to stay mindful, describing what you see, how you feel, and what you're doing can help bring you back to the present if you find your mind wandering. Imagine coming upon this moment out of the blue or from another planet. What would it look like from an outsider's perspective? What would someone who is not you see?

October 6

Letting go of the past will help you stay focused on the now. Of course, if letting it go were that easy, we'd all be perfectly present all the time. Today take a good, hard look at a memory of the past that's been weighing you down. Spend some time with it and then make the conscious choice to release it. Only you can let it go. Only you can set yourself free from the baggage of the past.

October 7

Be constantly curious. Wondering why will always encourage you to be more mindful. Asking questions and looking for the answers will bring you into the moment. Curiosity has so many positive benefits, but one of the greatest is its ability to keep alert to the world all around you.

October 8

Redirect your thoughts from what-could-be to what-is. Focus on what you're thinking instead of just letting your thoughts run wild. Learning to question your thoughts—rather than accept them as objective facts, which they are not—can have a huge impact on becoming more mindfulness. The future is a tempting place to visit, but it's no match for living in the moment. Keep your thoughts focused on the now.

October 9

When you've had a particularly good experience, it can be hard to move forward because you may feel as if you're losing a part of the experience with every passing moment. Just because you're living in the moment doesn't mean you're not conscious of the good things that happened in the past. Being present doesn't mean losing the best parts of your past; it simply means making the most of those memories right now.

October 10

Emotional baggage can get in the way of mindfulness. When your mind is clouded with negative thoughts, it is difficult to see the moment clearly. Clean out your emotional closet. Give away the things you do not need, the things weighing you down, the things out of date. With less weight on your mind, you'll be free to focus your attention on today.

October 11

Meditation can be a powerful ally when it comes to mindfulness. It doesn't necessarily require hours of sitting in a quiet room with your legs crossed and your heart chakra open. All you need are a few moments alone, a few deep breaths, and a space where you can clear your mind. The simple act of closing your eyes and taking a deep breath can bring you back to the present.

October 12

Pause right where you are, right now, and stay here in this moment. Don't let your mind wander back to the past and what was. Don't allow yourself to contemplate all the things that could be. This is the moment that's *real*. This is the moment that's *now*. It's the only thing that matters. Focus your attention on it. Be *here*. Be *now*.

October 13

One way to be mindful of the world around you is to be fully present when you're interacting with others. Really listen when someone is speaking to you. Pay attention not only to his or her words, but also to the body language, the tone, the potential meaning behind them. Try not to jump in and interrupt today. Let others speak and let yourself truly listen to what's being said.

October 14

Focus on one of your five senses today. Pick the one that resonates the most with you and spend the day being conscious of what you see / hear / taste / small / feel. All five of your senses are so important, but when you focus on one, everything you experience related to that one sense becomes more vivid. Colors will be more dazzling. Scents will be more prominent. Tastes will be more delicious. Textures will be more dynamic. Sounds will be more inspiring.

October 15

If you're waiting for your life to begin, today's the day you can stop waiting. What's meaningful—what you should be mindful of—is what's happening right now. This is it. *This is your life.* If you don't pay attention and give every moment the consideration it deserves, you'll miss it. Don't waste time looking around. Be present in your own life.

October 16

Picture a dog on a walk. What does she do? She stops and looks at everything. She smells (what seems like!) each blade of grass. She perks her ears at the slightest sound. Now imagine what it would be like to be a dog, to be so wrapped up in the moment that you are aware of everything happening around you. Dogs are not worried about what comes next; they don't dwell on what happened in the past. Today, try to live life as a dog would—fully embracing each moment.

October 17

Are you mindful of the words you speak? Too often, we speak without thinking. We say what we want without knowing if it's really what we want to say. Be mindful of your words today. Before you speak, consider what you want to say—and how you want to say it.

October 18

Attach the idea of mindfulness to a routine you do every day. For example, choose to embrace mindfulness when you're brushing your teeth. This is something you (hopefully!) do on a daily basis, and if you use it as a reminder for mindfulness, each and every day you'll be prompted to be present when you pick up your toothbrush. Find a daily routine—maybe even one you don't love so much—and use it positively to stay present.

October 19

Focus on one task at a time today. It can almost be impossible not to multitask these days, but try to avoid it whenever you can. Whatever you're doing today, do just that. Don't talk to others while you're doing it. Don't watch TV while you're doing it. Do one thing at a time today and heighten your awareness of every move you make.

October 20

Mindless eating is a dangerous thing. Not only can it cause you to gain unnecessary weight, but it can also prohibit you from truly enjoying the food you eat. Enjoy every meal you eat today. Better yet, enjoy every *bite*. Savor the foods you consume by eating slowly and paying close attention to what you're munching on. Even if you're not a foodie, you can appreciate various flavors and textures—if only you make the effort to be aware of them.

October 21

Focusing on yourself, your breathing, and your thoughts can make a big difference when it comes to being a more mindful person—but you have to make time for that focus. Try to spend five minutes today doing absolutely nothing. No people, no music, and no distractions. See where your mind goes—and make an effort to bring it back to the now.

October 22

To be mindful, you must become open-minded. You must push aside your judgments and your assumptions and let the moment be whatever it is. It is not easy to let go of ideas you've held on to for a long time, but today try to see the world— and the people in it—with an open mind. Rather than looking for what should be, pay attention to what is.

October 23

Strive to do less every day. A culture of hurry and rush makes it very difficult to be mindful. Prioritize what's truly important to you and find ways to get rid of the time you spend on unimportant activities. Mindfulness is hard work, and it doesn't work so well when you have a million and one things to be mindful of. Narrow your life down to the things that matter.

October 24

Don't hold back when it comes to experiencing joy. The next time something makes you feel really, really good, get into it and really embrace it. Pay attention to every emotion you're feeling and every shiver of delight that runs down your spine. True joy can be fleeting so capture the experience of it while you can and allow yourself to be fully present in your pleasure.

October 25

Life is sprinkled with little bits of magic. Even the mundane can be magical. Look for enchantment in your life today. Look for things that astound you. Pay attention to things that make you pause and say, "Wow. That's amazing." Many things in life defy explanation and exceed expectation. Make an effort to be mindful of all that magic.

October 26

Practice makes perfect, or so they say. This cliché happens to be oh-so-true when it comes to the art of mindfulness. Being fully present won't happen overnight—and it won't happen all the time. It takes work, but the more you practice it, the better you'll get at it. Don't give up on yourself, even when it's frustrating. Every moment is a chance to reconnect with mindfulness. Every second is a chance to be present.

October 27

Being mindful can be difficult, especially if you're not super excited about whatever you're getting into today, but if you make the extra effort to look around you—to really, truly pay attention to your life and all that surrounds you—you'll find that there's a lot to be excited about. Mindfulness keeps you present and helps keep unnecessary stress at bay. Pay attention to everything, even the tiny details, and you'll find that every moment is worth being mindful of.

October 28

Seeing life through a camera lens can do wonders for your state of mindfulness. Grab your camera (or your phone) and start looking for things to photograph. When you are on the hunt for a great photo, you are more aware of the world around you. What you might not have noticed before suddenly grabs your attention and seems interesting. Even when you don't have a camera handy, try to see the world as if you did. Look for life's many photo ops.

October 29

Look around the room you spend the most time in. What do you see? What would it be like to look at this place from an outsider's point of view? You spend so much time in the place that it might be difficult to see it through fresh eyes, but try. Today is the day to see your world—the parts closest to you—from a new viewpoint.

October 30

There are moments in which mindfulness comes more easily. In these moments, you are in the zone, in the flow of life, and you are focused on something that truly interests you. Pay attention to when you experience mindfulness effortlessly. These are the moments you should be making more of. Those are the activities you should be doing every single day. Doing what you love is the very best way to easily embrace the now.

October 31

Be mindful of the love in your life, of all the people you have to be grateful for. Those who love you are not a given. They are a gift. Treasure each moment you spend with your loved ones. Stop racing to cross things off your to-do list. Stop fretting about the work you have yet to do. Stop hurrying and scurrying and missing out on the best moments you have: the moments filled with scents and sounds and sights of those you love—and those who love you.

APPRECIATE THE AMAZING

Gratitude

November 1

Gratitude is essential not only for improving personal relationships, but for improving the world as a whole. Every word or act of gratitude ripples through the universe, spreading kindness and positivity. Having an attitude of gratitude is can change the lives of others—and your own life as well.

November 2

Think of gratitude not as an obligation or as something you should do, but as an act of love. It sounds a bit cheesy but, really, what is gratitude if not an act of love? Thankfulness—in whatever form—is a way to love someone else. When you love someone, you cannot help but incorporate gratitude into love. Today consider how you can incorporate love into gratitude.

November 3

How often do you say thank you and *really* mean it? How often do your tone and body language and the look in your eyes convey just how grateful you are? Make sure the gratitude you express is sincere. The words "Thank you" can seem so small, but if said in the right way, they can mean so much.

November 4

What are you most thankful for? Consider the things in your life you frequently take for granted—things like health and love and friendship. Pay attention to those things today and make an effort to acknowledge them more often. Often we don't realize what we have until it's gone. Choose to appreciate it now. Choose to appreciate all you have before it's too late.

November 5

Gratitude can sometimes slip through the cracks. You might feel it. You might mean to show it. But then you don't. And that's a dangerous thing. When you forget to show gratitude—even if you feel it—you are withholding something valuable, something that creates more positivity in the world. The next time you feel grateful, don't forget to express thankfulness out loud.

November 6

Expressing gratitude shouldn't always be about gifts, but a little trinket or a thoughtful card makes thankfulness come to life. Think of those who have done sweet things for you lately—those who have gone out of their way for you when they really didn't have to—and send those people thank you cards or buy each of them a treat they'll really enjoy. A little token of gratitude can be a really big deal.

November 7

When you're at your lowest, feeling your worst, that's when you need gratitude the most—and, of course, that's when it's the hardest to remember to focus on it! The next time you're feeling really low, remind yourself to be thankful. Take a time out from your stress or sadness and consider all the things you have to be thankful for.

November 8

To be more grateful for life, you must be more present in it. You must be still and pay attention to what is have all around you. You must be conscious of the things you do, the people you love, and the experiences you have. Everything matters. Every little thing in life is something to be thankful for.

November 9

To open your heart to gratitude, you must be kind to others. Do not be short-tempered or quick to judge. Do not move at such a lightning-fast speed that you forget the needs or desires of others. Slow down. Be kind—not only to others, but also to yourself.

November 10

Be thankful for your family—parents, children, cousins, aunts, uncles, siblings. They are such a constant presence in your life that you may take them for granted. Give special thanks for them today and tell each of them how much they mean to you. Even if it's hard to express your gratitude—or even if you don't feel very grateful in this moment—try to show those you love how thankful you are for them.

November 11

Embracing the positive aspects of your life will help you be more grateful. When you look at the bad, you'll see the bad and you'll become senselessly dissatisfied with life. When you look at the good, you'll see the good and you'll realize that this life really is a magical, wondrous experience filled with amazing things to see and do. Focus on the positive and gratitude becomes effortless.

November 12

Expand your heart and mind to all there is to be grateful for in this world. Keep an open mind when it comes to gratitude. The things you should appreciate are not always so obvious. Think outside the typical thankfulness box. Consider the little things—the things you might take for granted on a daily basis, like your hairbrush or running water—and celebrate them.

November 13

Giving is one of the best ways to show gratitude. And giving doesn't have to be about giving money. There are so many gifts—like the gift of joy or the gift of laughter—you can give every day. Show your gratitude with gifts. Give back to those who always give to you. Bestow gifts to those who have given you nothing.

November 14

Positive people are grateful people. Ungrateful people cannot be positive—or happy. Gratitude is vital to living a positive life because, without it, you cannot truly embrace the goodness of living. Gratitude is life affirming. It serves as a reminder of all the wonderful reasons it's great to be alive, to be *here*. When you choose to be grateful, you're choosing to live a positive life.

November 15

Even on the worst day, in the middle of the worst mood, gratitude can uplift you. When you find yourself between a rock and emotional hard place, consider all the things you have to be thankful for. Take out a blank piece of paper and make a list of all you have to be grateful for. The act of thinking thankfully can brighten even the darkest days.

November 16

Gratitude—just like positivity—is a choice. It will not always come easily. It will not always be obvious. But it is always an option. Look around you right now. What is good about your situation? What are you thankful for? You don't have to be thankful only for the good things in your life. Even the difficult things are worthy of gratitude because these things often make you stronger, smarter, *better*.

November 17

Gratitude is a great way to stay focused on the now. Instead of allowing your mind to fret about the future or dwell on the past, choose to focus on the things you are grateful for *right now* in this moment. There are many, many things right in the here and now that deserve your appreciation.

November 18

Ungratefulness leads to negativity. It creates an unappreciative atmosphere that can permeate any situation—no matter how positive. Pay attention to the words and actions of those around you. Are they grateful? Are they appreciative of all they have? Are they appreciative of *you*? Ungrateful people will pull you down. Don't let them drag you into negative—and ungrateful—territory.

November 19

Nothing makes a relationship better than when you are truly grateful for the other person. All relationships have ups and downs, but if you keep gratitude in mind no matter what you're going through, you're more likely to have a better, more positive relationship. The simple act of being thankful can improve any interaction.

November 20

Use gratitude to motivate yourself. Think about the abilities and talents you have and be thankful for them. Inspire yourself by reminding yourself of all you've been given. Being grateful can motivate you to believe in yourself, and it can also inspire you to see all you have to offer the world. Gratitude will make you aware of what you have to give.

November 21

Choose to make today a grateful day. Focus on thankfulness and appreciation. Look for all the ways—every tiny little thing—you can be thankful for. Drive people crazy by saying "thank you." Bring gratitude into the forefront of your life today. Focus on it intentionally, intensely and see how all that thankfulness makes you feel.

November 22

Imagine you lost all electricity today. Imagine life without the Internet, your phone, your television. Picture life without air conditioning or lights. Imagining the absence of all the things you probably take for granted will help you stay grateful for the things you use on a daily basis. Be thankful for that working light switch, that Internet browser. Be grateful for that running water, that microwave.

November 23

Feeling thankful really does feel good. It allows you to nurture positive thoughts and cultivate good relationships. Gratitude makes you glow. It makes you shine. The next time you are thankful—really, truly grateful—notice how you feel. Pay attention to your happy thoughts, your wide smile, and your open body language. Remember those good feelings the next time its tough to be thankful.

November 24

Say this out loud: "I am thankful for everything I have." You might not *feel* thankful, but saying those words will trigger some gratitude in you. When you speak those words aloud, you might realize that, yes, you really *are* thankful for everything you have. Speaking words of gratitude can help you connect with inner appreciation.

November 25

Consider your five senses. What if one of those senses no longer worked? What would it be like to be blind or deaf? Today spend a moment contemplating all the wonderful things you can see and hear and taste and touch and see. Be thankful for your five senses, for all the joy they bring you on a daily basis.

November 26

Go somewhere you've never been before (even if it's just a different street in your neighborhood). A new environment triggers awareness. Use that awareness to be thankful not only for the new things you're seeing—but all the new things and people and experiences you've yet to see. Be thankful for what's to come.

November 27

Keeping a gratitude journal is one of the best ways to cultivate an attitude of gratitude. Set aside a few moments at the end of each day to write down a few things you're grateful for. Doing this will not only give you a chance to reflect on gratitude at the end of each day, but it will also cause you to be more conscious of things you're grateful for all day long.

November 28

Choose appreciation instead of expectation when it comes to those you love. Instead of expecting things from others, consider the ways you can appreciate them and be grateful for them just as they are. Expectations can cause a great deal of pain and frustration—but appreciation never lets you down. It will always bring you—and your relationships—up.

November 29

When was the last time you were thankful for simply being you? Be thankful for yourself. Show yourself love and admiration. The person you are is wonderful and—just as you would with a friend or a loved one—you should be grateful for who you are, for what you bring to the world. Be thankful for *you*.

November 30

The next time you find yourself complaining, push those negative thoughts aside and make room for gratitude. Complaints never do you any good—in fact, they usually make you unhappier—but gratitude will navigate you to a place of positivity. When you find your mind filled with complaints, tell yourself, "It's time to stop grumbling and start being grateful!"

CHOOSE IT OR LOSE IT

Happiness

December 1

A positive attitude (accompanied by positive choices) leads to happiness. Every moment, every single second, is a chance to choose positivity and to give yourself a chance at being happy. Some of those moments will make the choice very difficult, but if you know a positive attitude is always an option, you'll always be open to finding happiness.

December 2

One cause of unhappiness is imagining the past as different than it really was. We often see the past through rose-colored glasses, envisioning it as a wondrous place that we wish we could go back to. Instead of creating a new, better version of the past in your mind, try to focus on the now. Yes, the past may have held some great times, but you will never be happy if you keep looking in the rearview mirror. Focus on the road in front of you. *That's* the path to happiness.

December 3

Want to be happy with who you are? Create a list of ten things about yourself that make you happy. You are not perfect—who is?!—but there are many amazing things about you. Focusing on what you love about yourself will give even the toughest of days a quick jolt of happiness. Self-love is a gateway to everlasting happiness.

December 4

Stress quickly drains happiness from your life. If you want to be happy, you have to avoid stress. Which means you have to stop worrying so much about what the future holds. Accept that things will work out—even if you can't see how they could possibly do that right now. Accept that you don't have control over everything and sometimes the best, most happiness-inducing thing you can do is let your worry go.

December 5

Oddly enough, happiness can be a scary thing. When you're happy, you might hold yourself back from truly experiencing pure joy because you think it might leave you or, worse yet, you think you don't deserve it. Don't hold back when it comes to happiness. You deserve every single drop of it. When happy moments come your way, drink 'em up. You deserve them.

December 6

What makes you happy? Consider this question carefully. Don't allow yourself to answer with what you think should make you happy or what you wish did make you happy. Spend time really indentifying the things, people, activities, and places that bring you happiness. And then ask yourself, "Do I have enough of these happy things in my life?"

December 7

Making others happy will almost always make you happy too. Today is a good day to go out of your way for someone you love (or maybe someone you don't even know!) and do something to make him or her happy. It doesn't have to be a big thing, but do at least one thing today that puts a smile on someone else's face.

December 8

Are you sabotaging your own happiness? Though blaming others is tempting, you are often the only one standing in the way you being happy. You have to allow yourself to be happy—and you also have to clear the way for happiness. If you want to be happy, you must embrace positivity. You must focus on the now. You must surround yourself with positive and mindful people.

December 9

Do you know what will make you happier than almost anything? Doing what you love. When you do what you love—that one thing you're *really* passionate about—you create a deep and lasting sense of happiness for yourself, a happiness that can be accessed whenever you do the thing that brings you joy. Do what you love as much as you can and happiness is sure to find you.

December 10

Allow yourself to really feel happiness. Push the doubts from your mind—the "what ifs" and the "buts"—and just let happiness lay down beside you. Let yourself relax by its side. There is something to be said for clearing your mind of all doubt and just letting yourself feel happy (even in the moments when it doesn't feel like you should be happy). Allow yourself a small but powerful moment of pure acceptance, of perfect happiness.

December 11

True happiness is wanting what you get. How often do you wish you had something else? Or wish you could be someone else? Instead of comparing and wishing, start accepting what you have. Happiness comes to those who are grateful and content. There will always be something just out of your reach—but the one thing that's always accessible to you is a positive attitude. Choose that and you choose a happier life.

December 12

Stop whatever you're doing and think about everything making you happy right now. Look around you. Contemplate the people in your life. Think of the things that have gone right over the past couple of days. Pausing and considering all the happy things in your life is a great way to work on having a positive attitude—and it's also an instant mood-booster!

December 13

Don't be lazy when it comes to happiness. It takes work to be happy—to take positive thoughts and turn them into a happy life—but all the effort you put into it will come back to you tenfold. The trick is not to give up, or give in. Negative thoughts will hound you. Unhappy people will surround you. Don't stop trying; don't stop being happy.

December 14

Are you in such a rush that you're missing out on happiness? You'll never see the good in life if you're always rushing past it. Make a conscious effort to slow down, to take pleasure in whatever you're doing. Slow down and take a look around. We're all on a highway, speeding along, but if you put on the brakes a little bit, you'll be able to see happiness everywhere.

December 15

If you want happiness in your life, you have to design a life that makes room for it. You are not in control of everything, but you do have a lot of control over what you say, do, and think. You also have control over who you surround yourself with and what you spend your time doing. Is your life a breeding ground for happiness? If not, consider what you could change to make it a place where happiness can grow and flourish.

December 16

Happiness is happiness, no matter how tiny it might seem. Even a little burst of happiness is worth enjoying. Don't limit yourself to what "should" be worth celebrating. Any happiness—teeny tiny or oh-my-god amazing—should be embraced and enjoyed. Treat every happy experience with exuberance because you never know which happy moment will be your last.

December 17

Don't be afraid to share your happiness with others. You might not want to seem like you're bragging or showing off, but one of the great things about happiness is *sharing* it. The people in your life will be happy to see you happy. (And if they're not happy for your happiness, you might be happier without them!) When something good happens, don't hold it in. Share it!

December 18

A happy life is not a perfect life. In order to be happy, you don't have to have everything in its place. You don't have to have everything figured out. Happiness is an emotion you can experience wherever you are, whenever you are. Don't fall into the trap of "I'll be happy when…" If you have that mentality, you'll *never* be happy. You'll just always be waiting for happiness. Remember: perfection isn't a requirement for happiness.

December 19

Relying on others to make you happy is a surefire way to find yourself very *un*happy. While, of course, others can bring you happiness, depending on them to do so will leave you in a pretty tough spot should something happen to them. Make your own happiness.

December 20

Happiness is a kind of generosity. When you're unhappy, you suck the life from other people. Your presence is draining, tiring. However, when you adopt a happy attitude, you give off an inspiring light, a light that can brighten others' dark days. When you're happy, you're giving something back to the people around you. When you're happy, you make the world a brighter, lighter place.

December 21

Happiness does not exist in some distant future. Happiness is *right now*. Right now, in this very moment, you can choose to be happy. Despite the troubles, the worries, the what-could-bes, you can choose to look at the positive aspects of life. You can choose to make yourself happy. Never forget that happiness is *now*.

December 22

Happiness is not a butterfly to be chased. It is not an external force to be pursued. It is a state of mind. It does not lie in money or relationships or fame. Happiness is within you. *Always*. It's just a matter of accessing it. If you must pursue happiness, pursue it within yourself. You don't have to chase the butterfly. You don't have to wait for the butterfly to land on you. You *are* the butterfly—living, free, and happy.

December 23

Being with the people you love (even the ones who get on your nerves sometimes!) is happiness. Even if you're not a people person, people can be a source of happiness. Make a conscious effort to spend quality time with someone who loves, supports, and uplifts you. The happiness that lies within you will be triggered by the positive power of spending time with someone you love.

December 24

If you want to be truly happy, you must stop avoiding unhappiness. The more you avoid unhappiness, the happier you'll be. Why? Because avoiding unhappiness (and all the negative emotions that come with it) takes a lot of energy and causes a lot of stress. Energy that could be spent on being happy goes to feeling sorry for yourself or worrying about your situation. Don't dwell on unhappiness, but don't avoid it either. Allow yourself to feel what you need to feel—and then direct your attention back to the positive things in your life.

December 25

Big bursts of happiness come when you celebrate. Celebrate holidays. Celebrate special occasions. Celebrate little victories. Life is filled with reasons to celebrate—and every time you pause and recognize those special moments you're not only celebrating that occasion, but you're also creating more happiness, more gratitude, and more positivity in your life. Celebrate every chance you get because you don't want to look back and wish you'd had more celebratory confetti, triumphant toasts, or holiday happiness.

December 26

One way to find the happiness within yourself is to spend your time doing things that are meaningful to you. A happy life is a purposeful life. When you feel you have a purpose—when you know what you're doing and why you're doing it—you are content with your day-to-day routine. Your life is filled with substance and that substance fills your heart and mind with endless amounts of happiness.

December 27

Don't habitually sacrifice your own happiness to please others. It's okay to compromise or occasionally do something you don't love to do to make someone else happy. But when you start sacrificing your own happiness for the sake of others on a regular basis, everyone loses. You lose because you are unhappy (and, ultimately, resentful). Others lose because you'll inevitably lash out at them for causing you unhappiness. Finding a balance between compromise and sacrifice is difficult, but it's essential for living a positive, happy life.

December 28

Are you truly happy or are you simply not unhappy? Yes, there's a difference. Happiness is a proactive thing, something you actively and purposefully choose, not an absence of something. When you are truly happy, you constantly access that happy place within yourself. You are in constant contact with your self and the world around you. Be honest when you ask yourself, "Am I really happy?"

December 29

The next time you find yourself feeling unhappy, find a mirror and give yourself a big, goofy grin (the sillier the better!). No matter how hard you resist, seeing yourself looking silly is bound to put a real smile on your face—and the sight of yourself smiling in the mirror will lift your spirits and make whatever challenges you're facing much more manageable.

December 30

Limiting yourself—emotionally, physically, or mentally—can put a damper on your happiness. When you allow yourself to believe that you can't change or push your own boundaries, you hold yourself back. You can both accept yourself as you are *and* refuse to limit yourself. Unfortunately it's often easier to set limits, but it's never a good way to bring happiness into your life. Life is filled with opportunities—and you'll be much happier if you stay open to them.

December 31

Change can bring about happiness, but so can staying the same. Instead of thinking back on the past year and contemplating how you want to be different next year, look back on the past 365 days and ask yourself, "What made me happy?" Focus on those happy moments and resolve to make those situations / people / experiences part of the year ahead. No matter what the next year brings, you deserve to live a positive and present life filled with heaps of happiness.

ABOUT THE AUTHOR

Danielle (also known as Dani) DiPirro is the creator of PositivelyPresent.com, a site dedicated to helping people around the world live more positive and present lives. Dani began her career in marketing before leaving her full time job to focus on her true passion, inspiring others through words. She lives in the suburbs of Washington, DC with her two great loves: her boyfriend and her dog. Find more inspiration from Dani here:

WEBSITE // PositivelyPresent.com

TWITTER // @positivepresent

FACEBOOK // facebook.com/positivelypresentdani

PINTEREST // pinterest.com/positivepresent

Made in the USA
Lexington, KY
02 July 2015